DYNAMIC
&
EFFECTIVE
VIRTUAL
TRAINING

Monica,
Hopefully THE IDEAS
IN THIS BOOK will HELP
WITH OUR NEW NORMALS
AND VIRTUAL MEETINGS
AND TRAINING. BEST WISHES
FOR 2020 AND BEYOND
Neil

CARA GOMEZ, EDD
NEIL CORDREY

DYNAMIC
&
EFFECTIVE
VIRTUAL
TRAINING

31 Strategies to Design and Facilitate Training in an Online Environment

RIDGE WATER PRESS

Ridge Water Press
PO Box 395
Clayton, DE 19938

ISBN 9798653250163

To Cindy C. and Rafael G. with love

Table of Contents

Introduction

You are a facilitator who conducts, or is preparing to conduct, virtual training courses. You may offer webinars, teach large training sessions, or coach small groups. Regardless, you know that while facilitating online training is similar to in person training, there are concerns specific to the virtual environment.

How do I ensure that the participants learn essential skills while training through a screen?

Can I keep the class engaged virtually for an entire day or week?

If I have a resistant attendee, how do I connect with them online?

Whether you are new to virtual training or have already been conducting online training and want to host dynamic and effective courses, this guide is for you.

The purpose of this guide is to teach you how to create virtual training courses that are dynamic, engaging, and effective.

After learning these principles,

- A trainer commented, "I am great at facilitating in-person sessions. I was very intimidated to convert my courses to a virtual setting. Using these strategies, I delivered my first online training session with confidence."
- A novice trainer said, "Before I learned these strategies, I could not get in front of anyone and talk. Now I do this for a living."
- A seasoned trainer observed, "I no longer fear the expert in the course or those who challenge me. The tools in this guide helped me to create confidence that I can handle any situation."
- Another trainer remarked, "Training used to be tedious, but I applied several of these ideas. Now I love training! My participants enjoy the courses too."

A dynamic training course should be engaging and enjoyable for the attendees. But training should also accomplish three other valuable objectives: increasing participants' knowledge or skills, changing their on-the-job behaviors, and improving business outcomes[1].

Training courses that do not meet all of these objectives are an underutilization of resources and time. This book includes thirty-one strategies for facilitating any virtual training course to create a positive impact on the participants' engagement, learning, behavior, and business-related results. The techniques presented in this guide model principles from the New World Kirkpatrick Model[1], Adult Learning Theories[2-4], Bloom's Taxonomy[5], and other best practice training principles.

You will be a dynamic facilitator in no time!

The purpose of this guide is to present principles to help you design and facilitate dynamic training across any virtual platform. There are no instructions on using specific Learning Management Systems (LMS) or programs. Depending on your organization, you may have no choice in the LMS or might be limited to the programs you can use. Regardless of the virtual delivery platform, you can apply the strategies in this guide to design and facilitate your course.

The Sections of This Guide

There are five sections in this guide. Each section contains several strategies vital for a dynamic virtual training course. The explanations are short and include several implementation ideas specific to an online setting.

Section 1 contains foundational principles for your course. These concepts establish the groundwork for the training that should underpin your design process and implementation. These strategies include how to keep participants' attention and use active learning techniques in the virtual environment.

Section 2 focuses on media and technology. There are specific ideas for choosing the appropriate technology to deliver the course and enhance participant engagement. Strategies in this section include application and software suggestions for course activities, ideal PowerPoint design, and social media use.

Section 3 outlines the online course design. This section discusses a comprehensive overview of planning a course, including pre-course communication, session planning, and the follow-up period. Specific strategies included in this section are opening with a bang, organizing the learning process, and conducting effective debriefing.

Section 4 discusses personal facilitation techniques. You can modify live presentation skills for online delivery. These strategies focus on avoiding silence and adapting to learning preferences in a virtual environment.

Section 5 concentrates on engaging participants. Facilitators can uncover the underlying reasons why participants may be disengaged or resistant to the learning process. Even in a virtual setting, facilitators can minimize participant resistance and build trust to optimize training effectiveness.

How to Use This Guide

Is Your Course Already Designed? If you have already designed your virtual course, read through this guide in its entirety before making any modifications. Write out your answers to the 'Apply This Strategy' questions at the end of each strategy. Choose two to three focus areas to modify the next time you facilitate your course. You can quickly implement simple techniques from Section 2 (Using Technology and Media), Section 4 (Implementing Personal Facilitation Effectiveness), and Section 5 (Minimizing Facilitation Inhibitors) without restructuring your entire course. Gradually incorporate other strategies each time you run your course.

Are You Preparing to Design Your Course? If you are in the early design stages, read through the entire guide first. Thinking about your specific content, answer the "Apply This Strategy" questions to prompt ideas for your course creation. Focus primarily on Section 1 (Establishing Facilitation Foundations), Section 2 (Using Technology and Media), and Section 3 (Organizing the Learning) to plan your content and delivery. A flowchart for constructing your course can be found in Strategy 24 (Structure Your Course: Putting It All Together).

Are You Flipping Your Course Quickly? It would be difficult to apply all of these strategies if you have to quickly adjust your training from in-person training to a virtual learning environment. If you are abruptly converting your course, start with Strategy 7 (Choose your Technology and Applications), Strategy 5 (Keep Their Attention in A Virtual Setting), and Strategy 6 (Use Active Learning Exercises) for quick ideas to employ technology and embed active learning. Modify two to three aspects of your course each time you teach as you have time. Assess what is working and what you should adjust.

Implementation Tools

There are three appendices to help you implement the strategies in this guide.
- **Appendix A** contains a checklist that is useful for planning or reviewing a course design.

- **Appendix B** includes a checklist you can use to evaluate your facilitation style.
- **Appendix C** consists of a continuous improvement reflection for ongoing review as you implement your courses.

In this guide, each strategy contains many examples. Some suggestions are better suited for synchronous (live sessions where everyone is participating simultaneously) or for asynchronous (pre-recorded and self-paced material) delivery. However, you can use many of the suggestions regardless of the delivery model. Some activities are better suited for courses with few participants, but you will see modification suggestions for larger class sizes. You can view the examples as a creative springboard and adjust the ideas to fit your content and delivery strategy.

Do not try to use every example in each strategy for your course! Choose the suggestions that will accentuate your material and create a dynamic learning environment for your course.

Being an engaging facilitator in a virtual environment is a skill. The strategies are presented in short chapters and are easy to implement. Try incorporating a few at a time. Use the continuous improvement model (see Appendix C) to implement, review, and improve. You will be a dynamic and effective trainer in no time!

Section 1: Establishing Facilitation Foundations

Strategy 1: Start with the End

The first thing to do when planning to facilitate any type of training is to start with the END. Identifying the intended organizational outcomes is especially important for a virtual course design. The type of technology you choose, the total length of the training, and the activities you incorporate are dependent on the purpose of the training. Determine the end goal by asking this question: WHY are the participants attending the training?

If the end goal is simply to provide participants with a certificate of completion, press the decision-makers to provide a more in-depth answer. Training for the sake of training is simply busywork for both facilitators and employees. Does the company want to improve safety outcomes? Provide exceptional customer service? Increase productivity? Decrease waste? Decrease employee turnover? The company most likely invested in the training to impact a business metric. That is the "end." Before you do any planning, start with the end and **find the why.**

You should then consider: What changes in employee behavior are necessary to impact that business metric? Behavioral changes often occur by increasing an employee's knowledge, skills, or confidence levels.

After determining the why, you need to figure out WHAT behaviors the employees need to change and WHAT knowledge or skills they need to learn to change those behaviors.
WHAT the participants must learn is referred to as "learning objectives." Learning objectives should be written with clear and concise action verbs that can be demonstrated and measured.

Insert your learning objectives into a sentence like this:

By the end of this course, the participant will be able to

Poor learning objectives include the following:
- *Learn* about the types of machinery in the plant
- *Understand* the new hiring process
- *Know* the difference between our supply chain procurements
- *Appreciate* the brand equity theory as it relates to marketing

Learn, understand, know, and appreciate are difficult to demonstrate or measure. Instead, the following action verbs would be examples of better learning objectives:
- *Describe* the type of machinery in each plant
- Accurately *complete* the hiring process protocol in the online portal
- *Differentiate* between our supply chain procurements
- *Create* company logos using the brand equity theory

In the examples above, the verbs *describe, complete, differentiate, and create* can all be demonstrated and objectively assessed.

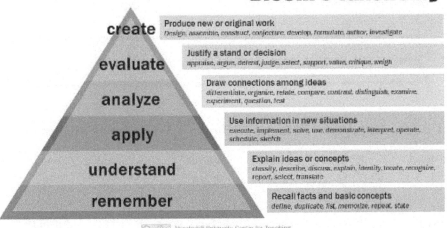

Bloom's Taxonomy

create — Produce new or original work
Design, assemble, construct, conjecture, develop, formulate, author, investigate

evaluate — Justify a stand or decision
appraise, argue, defend, judge, select, support, value, critique, weigh

analyze — Draw connections among ideas
differentiate, organize, relate, compare, contrast, distinguish, examine, experiment, question, test

apply — Use information in new situations
execute, implement, solve, use, demonstrate, interpret, operate, schedule, sketch

understand — Explain ideas or concepts
classify, describe, discuss, explain, identify, locate, recognize, report, select, translate

remember — Recall facts and basic concepts
define, duplicate, list, memorize, repeat, state

Vanderbilt University Center for Teaching

Bloom's Taxonomy is a framework to categorize learning objectives[5]. Participant learning outcomes can fall into categories described as remembering, understanding, applying, analyzing, evaluating, and creating.

Below is a table with a list of commonly used learning verbs that associate with each category in Bloom's framework[7,8]. You can use these verbs to write the learning objectives for your training course. All of the ones listed below can be converted into online activities or assessments using a variety of technological applications and platforms. This list of verbs will also spark ideas for active learning exercises (see Strategy 6) to use in your course to engage learners and accelerate the learning process.

Consider the participants' expertise when choosing the learning objectives for your course. Are you training participants who are new to the position or have a lower level of experience with the content? Then some of your initial learning objectives should be remembering, understanding, and applying outcomes. If your participants already have significant experience, consider beginning with analyzing, evaluating, or creating learning objectives.

By the end of my course, participants will be able to_____

Active Learning Verbs Relating to Bloom's Taxonomy Categories[7-8]

Remember	Understand	Apply	Analyze	Evaluate	Create
Answer	Cite	Articulate	Analyze	Criticize	Adapt
Define	Classify	Calculate	Contrast	Reframe	Change
Describe	Compare	Categorize	Connect	Judge	Collaborate
Duplicate	Contrast	Change	Relate	Defend	Compile
Identify	Demonstrate	Complete	Devise	Appraise	Construct
Illustrate	Discuss	Connect	Correlate	Value	Create
Label	Estimate	Construct	Illustrate	Prioritize	Design
List	Explain	Discover	Distill	Plan	Develop
Locate	Express	Integrate	Conclude	Grade	Elaborate
Match	Extract	Model	Categorize	Reframe	Improve
Memorize	Generate	Organize	Take Apart	Build	Innovate
Name	Indicate	Perform	Appraise	Appraise	Invent
Quote	Infer	Practice	Infer	Argue	Modify
Recall	Infer	Relate	Integrate	Convince	Modify
Recite	Interpret	Simulate	Structure	Deduct	Pivot
Recognize	Paraphrase	Sketch	Examine	Structure	Plan
Reproduce	Predict	Solve	Investigate	Measure	Produce
Retrieve	Relate	Teach	Research	Recommend	Rewrite
Select	Show	Transfer	Select	Validate	Role-Play
Tell	Summarize	Use	Differentiate	Interpret	Write

Lower Level Thinking Skills   Higher Level Thinking Skills

Chart adapted from Schinkel (2019)[8]

Be creative with choosing the action verbs for your learning outcomes. Make sure they align with the purpose of the course.

Conclusion

Begin with the end. Ask why the course is needed. Then determine what learning outcomes the participants must master. Learning objectives should be written using action verbs and are determined by participants' expertise. Active learning strategies can be developed around the learning outcomes to engage participants. Engaged learners participate in the learning process and are more apt to apply course content outside of the training. Sustained behavioral changes lead to improvements in business metrics—the end goal of the training.

Apply This Strategy

- Circle one to two learning objectives from each category of the framework that your participants would need to master in your course.
- Finish this sentence: "By the end of my class, the participants will be able to _____.

Strategy 2: Remember It Is Not About You

You are the one designing the virtual training. *You* have created the sessions. *You* are facilitating the class. *You* are the host of the virtual learning environment.

It may feel that all eyes are on you. You may feel the need to prove what you know and how well you know it.

But dynamic facilitators are aware of this fact: **It is not about you**. Outstanding training is not about your performance. Instead, exceptional training occurs when participants apply what they have learned in their work setting.

Does that relieve some pressure?

If you are facilitating a training session, you might fit into one or more of these categories:
- Someone who is a content expert or technical expert
- Someone who has to "train" participants who have more expertise than you
- Someone with some experience with the content but feel they have more to learn
- Someone who is intimidated to adapt to virtual training

To the Experts:
For all of you who are content experts: Remember, *it is not about you*. The goal of training is not to demonstrate how much you know. The goal is to find ways to support your attendees to master the learning objectives. On the virtual stage, it can be easy to approach training as a production. Instead, focus on your trainees and meet them where they are in the learning journey. Scaffold the delivery of your information. The participants may not grasp the information as quickly as you. They may

9

learn differently than you. Concepts that are obvious to you may be difficult for them to conceptualize. Become a learner-focused facilitator (see Strategy 28). Focus less on being the "sage on the stage" and more of a "guide on the side."

To Those Training Experts:
If you are nervous because there are participants with more expertise than you, it is ok! Remember: *it is not about you*. Think through the session objectives and how you can facilitate an environment to enable those experts to meet the course objectives. Several strategies in this guidebook explain activities you can use to draw out their expertise as you guide them toward the learning objectives (see Strategy 30)

To Those Who Feel They Have More to Learn:
Do you feel like you have some experience with the content, but there is much more you would like to learn before being comfortable teaching others? Your organization likely asked you to facilitate the training because you do have knowledge that will help the participants. And remember—*it is not about you*. The goal as a trainer is to guide learners to master the learning objectives. It is acceptable if there is more you need to know (in fact, most people are continually learning)! But for the course you are currently facilitating, work on designing an experience –with the knowledge you do have—to help the class learn. If you have participants with some expertise, review the learning objectives in Strategy 1. Choose learning objectives that involve evaluating, analyzing, or creating outcomes to challenge experienced participants and help them process new ideas. You can also use active learning exercises (see Strategy 6) in the virtual setting and shift the learning process towards the participants.

A Note to Those Intimidated by Virtual Learning
There is good news! This guide contains many practical and easy ideas to structure your online training course. And while there is a learning curve when using different types of technology and applications, remember—*it*

is not about you! You may experience technical glitches as you begin. Strategy 29 contains suggestions for diffusing awkward situations when presenting. Initially, focus on a simple course execution. Find uncomplicated methods to help the participants meet the learning objectives. You will become more comfortable each time you present.

Be the Guide on the Side

Conclusion

Training is not about being the "sage on the stage;" instead, you should see yourself as the "guide on the side." Guide your participants towards increasing knowledge and changing behaviors. You have met your training objectives when the participants have met their learning objectives. You may feel intimidated to train experienced attendees. Working in a virtual environment may initially feel awkward. Remembering that 'it is not about you' can keep your focus on the learner and enable you to design a dynamic course to meet their needs.

Apply This Strategy
- Do you feel you have to "be on stage" or "entertain" your participants?
- What is the most intimidating factor you face when facilitating a course? How can the principle "It's not about you" help mitigate that intimidation?
- Write a note reminding yourself to be the "guide on the side" and not on the center of the stage.

Strategy 3: Set-Up a Distraction-Free Environment

While you are trying not to be the "sage on the stage" (see Strategy 2), you are responsible for setting the virtual stage for the learning experience. You want to deliver a polished course as professionally as possible. Misspelled words, fonts that are difficult to read, and broken links take the participants' attention away from your content. You want your course design and implementation to be as distraction-free as possible. The students' focus should be on learning the course objectives. Glaring errors can cause distractions or difficulty navigating the course. Eliminate virtual distractions from your class by looking through the suggestions below and evaluating your materials.

Decrease Distractions in the Set-Up:
- Make sure there are no spelling or grammatical mistakes on any PowerPoint slides, video, multimedia, assignment instructions, email, or the Learning Management system.
- Keep the color palate uniform across learning materials.
- Use consistency with fonts, font colors, and font sizes.
- Check that font sizes are readable. Avoid huge and tiny fonts. Avoid fonts that are difficult to read.
- If using slides, make sure the PowerPoint or slide deck does not have a busy background. Make sure the font contrasts well with the slide background and is easily readable.
- Check your camera angle. You want to be looking straight ahead as much as possible (not looking down or up into the camera. Use a box or tripod to adjust device height.
- Make sure there is no glare behind you.
- Think about your background. Clear out a corner of a room where you record. Organized and uncluttered wall space can make a good background. On some video and recorded applications, you can choose a virtual video background. Choose one that is not busy or gaudy.

- Determine if you need additional lighting where you will be live or recorded. Do you need to open curtains to get more natural light? Add light bulbs? Purchase a soft studio light?
- Make sure all instructions are easy to follow.
- Check that all links and videos work.
- Practice navigating through the programs you are using so you are not fumbling during a session.
- Write clear and concise instructions on course documents. Provide links, passwords, and tutorials where needed.

Create a distraction-free course

Reduce Distractions When Conducting Sessions:
- Know where your camera is and talk toward the camera.
- Reduce distracting noise. Turn off your cell phone or alarms. Turn off alert sounds and notifications on your recording device.
- Let others know you are recording to prevent interruptions.
- Just as when you are presenting in person, take note of any distracting movement you might do. Try to avoid tapping fingers on a table, bouncing your legs, or any other repetitive motions that would show on the screen.
- Use a tripod or set the device on a sturdy surface to keep the recording steady.
- Make sure you have all the materials, links, websites, and activities prepared ahead of time.

Conclusion

You want the learner focused on your material and not sidetracked by distractions. You can eliminate distractions by carefully reviewing documents and making content look professional. Carefully choosing your background, looking toward the camera, and reducing background noise are strategies you can use to minimize distractions while presenting.

Apply This Strategy

- Decide where you will record. Make a mock five-minute video presentation and review it. Assess: How does the lighting look? Can you improve the background? Can you hear yourself well? Do you make any repetitive motions?
- Have a friend or colleague review the pre-course documents and session materials. Can they follow all of the instructions easily? Do all of the links and passwords work? Were any of the instructions confusing to them?

Strategy 4: Create a Welcoming Atmosphere

Have you ever logged into a webinar or training call, and sat there for five minutes in awkward silence while others logged in?

A training session or webinar starts the moment the first participant joins.

One role of the facilitator is to make participants feel comfortable. Simple activities starting from when the participants first join the class can reduce tension within the group. For some courses, this means making the participant feel welcome from the very first pre-course communication.

Some of your participants will join with a level of stress. Another role of the facilitator is to reduce their stress so they can focus on learning.

The class starts the moment the first participant logs in

Below is a list of ideas to create a welcoming environment for your class. Some suggestions are simple and easy but can be very successful.

- Play upbeat music as people are logging in or returning from break.
- Post a slide that says, "Welcome to Class!"
- Make a fun logo for the class. Put it on the Learning Management System, slides, and other training documents.
- Play a memorable jingle when a session is about to start, returning from a break, or pulling participants back from an active learning activity (see Strategy 6)
- Introduce yourself by having slides that present information about yourself or the class. Put the information in a multiple-choice question format. Using animation tools, have incorrect answers

drop off every couple of seconds until only the correct answer remains on the slide.

- Introduce yourself and welcome the first participant who logs in. Tell them it is their job to introduce themselves and welcome the next participant who logs in and to pass on instructions for that next participant to do the same.
- Create a slide deck of short bits of information relevant to the content of your course and set it on a scrolling loop while participants login. It can include related data, pictures, quotes, or more.

Conclusion

Investing in a short welcome can have significant dividends by reducing awkwardness and stress at the beginning of a course. Play music, create a jingle, or add a welcome slide as the participants log in. Find a creative way to introduce yourself to the group.

Apply this Strategy

- What do you currently do as people log into your course? Or, what do they first see when they start an asynchronous course?
- Choose a creative way to introduce yourself to the class as they log in.

Strategy 5: Keep Their Attention in a Virtual Setting

Are you worried participants will walk away from your lecture or not pay attention? When you are in a small in-person group, it is usually easier to help the attendees stay focused. But how do you engage participants in a virtual setting where there are other distractions? Adding quick interactions as you present will keep your participants' attention.

First, you can keep your talking or lecturing (passive learning) in segments of five to ten minutes. Then transition into an active learning activity (see Strategy 6). Not every active learning exercise has to take a long time—asking the participants to respond to a poll or choosing names for a discussion can keep participants engaged. Throughout the session, build in some of the longer active learning activities. Alternating passive and active learning techniques will keep the group focused.

If you are delivering an asynchronous class, this principle applies as well. Record your lecture in short segments and use your LMS to add activities or assignments. Some activities should be quick; others can be more in-depth. You can build modules where you can deliver a short video or lecture and intersperse quiz questions or write-in response questions throughout in some LMS and educational software. If you are going to have longer presentations, interjecting short activities keeps the learners engaged and increases the likelihood they will finish the video[9].

Second, during the time you are talking, intersperse short re-direct narratives to keep the participants' attention. Stories, multi-media, and object lessons are simple but powerful methods to help the group maintain focus.

Last, add elements such as music and quotes in your welcomes and transitions. These small actions complement the material and keep the attendees engaged.

Consider adding a few of these ideas to your course:

- Use music when participants log into the class or when they come back from a break. If you are creative, find a song that relates to the session content.
- Scroll slides that contain quotes that relate to the topic at the beginning of the session.
- Provide a course agenda or roadmap in an outline or graphic form (see charting example in Strategy 9). Keep the audience aware of where you are on the roadmap by showing a slide or screen share of the roadmap at the beginning of the day and refer to it each time you start a new section.
- Intersperse the session with two or three stories. Start a compelling anecdote at the beginning of the class and leave the participants hanging. Finish the story later in the course.
- Use a few objects that connect to parts of your session. Place them in a prominent area in your video screen near you but do not explain them right away. When the information is relevant, make the connection between that object and the content.
- Download or use a picture as your background. At the beginning of your session, hint that your virtual video background has significance. Do not explain the importance until later when it connects to your topic.
- Include one or two relevant video clips in your presentation. Clips can be from television shows, movies, or advertisements related to your industry or content that either illustrate a point or show a poor example. These clips can also provide a segue into a discussion or activity.
- If you take a break, give a teaser to create anticipation for the participants to return. For example: "When we return, we will uncover three secrets to unleashing employee potential." Teasers also work well at the end of a module to create excitement about the next topic. News channels apply this technique well.

- Conduct short quizzes throughout the sessions or lectures to keep the group focused.
- Use polling features or applications to conduct quick polls. You may want to use this information to tailor your examples or adjust content (see Strategy 28).
- Provide several questions to the group before a session so they can focus on the topic.
- Give a trivia quiz. List ten trivia questions related to your content on the screen share and get participants to write down their answers at home. Periodically throughout the session, ask someone to give their answer.
- Provide the group with a set of pictures related in some manner to your content. Throughout the course, share the images. Some video conference platforms allow participants to "raise their hand." Ask the first person to identify the picture and raise their hand to provide a connection between the image and the session content.
- Using video chat and screen sharing, ask for a volunteer. Give them instructions to complete a short task relating to your content. For example, ask a volunteer to make faces of a variety of emotions (or provide them a list of emotions). Screenshot the facial expressions. Then, use those pictures to discuss reading verbal and non-verbal cues in the workplace. This short activity will grab and hold participants' attention much more than providing a PowerPoint with facial expression clipart you found yourself.
- Use PowerPoint but mostly to only accentuate your session with pictures or diagrams. Do not read off your PowerPoints (see Strategy 8).

- If you need to share technical data, focus on a few slides at a time, and then shift to something else to keep their focus high.

Intersperse short re-direct activities to keep the participants' attention

---

Conclusion

Do not let participants hide silently behind their screens. Quizzes and polls help participants focus on information as you are talking. You can use stories and objects as teasers. Help your audience follow your session with a road map. Asking participants to raise a hand or volunteer breaks up a lecture segment. Small interactions throughout your presentation keep the audience engaged.

Apply This Strategy
- Reflect on a speech or a lecture you enjoyed. Which of the ideas above did the presenter use to keep the audience's attention?
- Think about your content. What is a television show that may have relevant clips you could use?

Strategy 6: Use Active Learning Exercises

There are books and a large body of research on how to incorporate active learning into the instructional design as it is one of the most effective tools to engage participants,[10] enhance learning,[11] and increase memory.[12] Active learning encourages students to make personal connections with the content and to learn through doing instead of listening. Active learning consists of guided activities that involve doing, discussing, and creating. While these may seem incongruous with virtual training, there are many creative ways to include active learning in an online setting.[13]

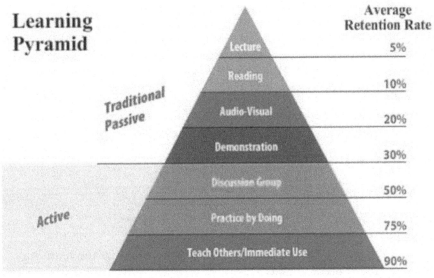

Source: NTL Institute for Applied Behavioral Science, Bethel, Maine , 1954[14]

The paragraphs below differentiate between passive and active learning. Following is a list of suggestions for conducting active learning exercises in a virtual environment. The activities are categorized based on Bloom's learning outcome framework.[7]

Passive Learning

Passive learning is a one-way presentation from an instructor to the participants. With passive learning, the instructor "pushes" the material toward the participants. Students passively engage with the content by listening or watching. The most common passive learning method occurs when participants listen to someone lecture or watch a recorded PowerPoint presentation. Reading or viewing demonstrations are also passive learning methods. These teaching techniques are good methods to explain concepts, skills, or ideas. There are times to use this approach, but it does not have to be the only choice, even in a virtual environment.

Active Learning

Active Learning involves the participants directly in their learning process. With active learning, participants discuss, write, draw, solve problems, practice, or teach. It causes them to use critical thinking skills and to apply the content to their world. This method is also sometimes referred to as a "pulling" method. The goal of active learning is not busywork; rather, active learning should be a conduit to guide students to make meaningful connections regarding the course material themselves.

As indicated in the learning pyramid, the retention rate of active learning methods are higher than passive learning methods. Teaching or immediately using the information results in the highest retention. Incorporating active learning into your training enhances the learning experience.

Most corporate training follows a passive model. However, dynamic facilitators alternate between active and passive approaches as they "push" small amounts of information to the class and then "pull" or provide several active learning activities to allow the participants to master the content.

A warning: It takes more energy to create an active session than a passive lecture. However, the results are worth the investment. Are you willing to put in the effort to design an outstanding training session?

You can use the extensive list of verbs in the Learning Outcomes Chart in Strategy 1 to create active learning exercises. Below are some ideas on how to execute activities in the virtual environment. You can adapt the examples based on your specific application, LMS, class size, and delivery method.

Remembering Activities
- Use polling apps or quiz applications. Some applications will allow participants to write in answers or complete true/false or multiple choice answers.
- Have students create quizzes for each other.
- Create a hotspot quiz. Hotspot quizzes require participants to click on a specific area of an uploaded picture. Hotspot quizzes are useful for labeling or identifying activities (e.g., Participants need to be able to identify safety cutoff switches on machinery).
- Use live video conference applications to have participants "raise hands" to answer questions. You can also permit students to ask questions to each other ("can you stump a colleague?").
- Make a "Who Wants to Be a Millionaire" type question list. Allow the participant in the hot seat to "phone a friend" or "poll the audience."
- Instruct participants to answer a question by making a list on paper or a virtual whiteboard. They can use a screen share to show the class. For example: Ask the participants to list all of the presented cues to use when providing employee feedback.

Understanding Activities

- Allow time for participants to discuss an idea. Start by calling on one participant. When they finish, they have to pick another name off of the video conference list to add to the discussion. That person then selects the next person to talk.

- Facilitate a "Think-Pair-Share" in a virtual environment. Ask a question and allow participants time to write down their answers. Use virtual breakout rooms in your video conference program to assign pairs. Give them time to discuss the questions and then bring everyone back together for a group discussion.

- Use live video or recorded videos to demonstrate a skill. Instruct the participants to practice the competency, then perform via a live video or recording. If applicable, you can ask the participant to explain what they are doing as they complete each part of the task. They can provide a rationale and specific details for each step. Several free applications permit quick video sharing between instructors and learners.

- Provide a question or problem. Use a chat feature or open-ended response question in a quiz builder for participants to type in an estimate or predict an outcome.

- Conduct a Six Thinking Hats[15] discussion activity using virtual backgrounds. In the Thinking Hats activity, participants all put on the same colored "hat" to discuss the idea from the same perspective. Present an idea, initiative, or project. Change your background color, or instruct all participants to change their backgrounds, as you guide the discussion. Use white to discuss the facts and available data on the topic; red to discuss their personal feelings or emotions about the issue and possible stakeholder reactions; black to discuss the downside, cons, and unintended consequences; yellow to discuss the pros; green to consider creative alternatives or other solutions; and blue to discuss the next steps or process needed to complete the project.

Applying Activities

- Ask participants to build a model out of household or office supplies
- Use screen share and stylus/writing apps for participants to sketch, write, or draw and share with the group.
- Provide a problem on your screen share. Allow participants to work through the problem on their device or paper, and then use screen share to explain their answer (they could also respond via a video).
- Provide real-world data sets to the participants. If the participants need a specific program, make sure each participant has a login. Provide questions or problems and let the participants work through the data to arrive at a solution. Some video chat programs will allow smaller "breakout" groups, where you can assign participants to work together in smaller groups.
- Assign content area to participants. Allow them fifteen minutes to "teach" their concept to the class. Encourage them to lecture or use a passive learning strategy (video/reading) for five minutes and then to incorporate an activity learning strategy for the last ten minutes.

Analyzing Activities
- Provide a video clip, article, news report, logo, or other item and allow students time to analyze it. You can ask them to create a checklist or rubric that they would use to assess this item. Have them compare documents to see others' ideas.
- Provide two (or more) objects, stories, or concepts. Using a shared document, ask students to describe the connections between the two things.
- Give students a topic related to the content of the session. Ask them to google an image associated with the content.

- Ask participants to illustrate a point or idea using any graphic design program.
- Present a real-world problem that occurs in your industry. Ask the participants to research new stories, data, or research articles related to the topic.

Evaluating Activities
- Using a chat feature, provide a statement or discussion starter. Instruct the participants to use respectful comments, and allow them to argue or convince each other of their viewpoint. Chat features that show running replies and sub-replies provide a better conversation environment than systems where participants have to click into and out of links to view the discussion.
- Provide the students with a website, project proposal, innovation, or something else related to the content of the course. Ask them to evaluate it and provide concrete details to justify their decision. You can ask them what would make it a better or stronger idea or item.
- Take an idea or topic that has two sides. Assign one participant to one viewpoint of the issue and another participant to an opposing view (regardless of their personal opinions). Have them each present an argument that supports their view through video chat.
- Play Family Feud. Assign half the participants to one side of an issue. They take turns in order listing arguments justifying that viewpoint until they have three passes. Give them a point for justification they make. Then if anyone from the other team has an additional view that the first team did not mention, they steal the points. Switch viewpoints for the next group. One significant aspect of this game is that it compels everyone to see the issue from the same angle for a few minutes regardless of their personal opinions.
- Do a "suggestion box" activity. Tell the students something you want to accomplish (decrease work-related safety incidences at the plant; increase productivity in a specific unit, etc.). Have the

participants write a recommendation letter outlining specific ways to accomplish this and email it to you or submit to an assignment link.

Dynamic facilitators use a mix of active and passive learning activities

---

Creating Activities

- Using a graphic program, have participants create a brochure, infographic, one-page marketing handout, poster, or sign related to your content. For example, have participants in a community safety course make public awareness posters for a current public health campaign.
- Have students produce a voiced-over PowerPoint or instructional video to "teach" the course-related content to departments within the company.
- Ask participants to research best practices as it relates to the content of your course. Instruct them to create a plan to implement those practices in their unit.
- Conduct a virtual brainstorming session. Tell the participants you want an innovative solution to a problem or issue related to the course content, your industry, or your specific organization. Tell the participants there are no right or wrong answers, and you will write down all answers regardless of feasibility. Type or use a stylus to write on your device as participants throw out all sorts of ideas. Encourage interdisciplinary ideas.
- Have students create a Public Service Announcement, short podcast episode, or even a song related to course content. Artistic content can be thoughtful and professional, such as a product you

would use at your organization. You can also encourage fun, nonsensical submissions as well!

The ideas above are to give you a starting point for designing active learning in your course. You can use ideas from one category and adapt it for learning outcomes in another.

Active learning often takes longer than passive content delivery. Therefore, you don't want to over-plan your exercises. Give participants time to complete the activity. You can use online timers to set time limits and pace your session.

A dynamic facilitator makes use of time before and after the actual sessions (see Strategy 7). Some of the activities do not need to occur during the course. Pre-work and follow-up projects create opportunities to expand learning beyond instructional time. You could assign review, factual information, and memory assignments with pre-course communication (see Strategy 12). For example, you can assign participants to review and provide suggestions for updating a training checklist for a piece of machinery. One of the activities during the next session would be for participants to discuss their modifications with others in the course. You can assign reflection and application activities as part of your course follow-up (see Strategy 22).

Conclusion

Active learning is a valuable component of successful training. You can implement many types of active learning exercises, even in the virtual setting, with a little creativity and technology. Strategically plan activities that align with your learning outcomes. Conduct activities to have participants recall, understand, analyze, evaluate, apply, and create information. Use the pre-course communication and follow-up period to expand learning beyond the instructional period.

Apply This Strategy

- Think of a recent course you attended. What is one thing you remember? Was it taught passively or actively?
- What percentage of that training was active? What percentage was passive?
- Describe how the facilitator of the training you attended could have used active learning exercises.
- Have you created a virtual learning training course already? Pick one idea above to add to your session. Are you planning to create a virtual learning course? What is one idea from the list above that you would like to incorporate?

Section 2: Using Technology and Media

Strategy 7: Choose Your Technology and Application Platforms

To design your training course in a virtual environment, you must choose the technology platform for your delivery. The type of platform and supplemental applications will depend on several factors:
- The purpose of the training (the why)
- The number of participants
- The level of simultaneous participant interaction
- Available learning management systems
- Budget for software and applications

The Purpose of the Training

Always start with the end. The principal factor to consider is WHY. WHY is the course being taught? What is the purpose of the training? What skills or learning objectives must the participants meet by the end of the course? WHY does the organization want employees to gain those skills? The answer to these questions should affect the remaining factors. For example, if you need participants to demonstrate specific skills, you most likely will want to limit the number of participants in each course, and you will need to choose video conference or video recording capabilities in your technology options.

The Number of Participants

After pinpointing the WHY of the course, consider how many participants you will serve each time you offer the course. The number of participants will affect the technology you may choose as your delivery system. Free learning and technology platforms may have a limit to the number of participants. If you know you may exceed the threshold of people to be eligible for a free service, you will either need to limit the number of attendees or the organization will need to invest in the platform.

Synchronous or Asynchronous

Synchronous and asynchronous courses refer to whether participants are conducting work simultaneously or on individual schedules.

Will all participants log in at the same time? Will they all watch and engage in activities simultaneously? Participants working and listening together is considered synchronous course delivery.

Will you post pre-recorded videos and instructions and allow participants to work through the material at their own pace? Self-paced learning occurs in an asynchronous course.

Delivery Platform or Learning Management System

To conduct an online course, you have to determine which technology you will use to deliver your course. Synchronous courses can use video conferencing technology. Asynchronous courses will need a "home" for the recorded lectures, modules, instructions, and participant activity submission. Your organization may pay for a specific LMS or use a free cloud-based system to house these files. Synchronous courses may also utilize an LMS to accommodate course documents, instructions, or resources.

Technology and Applications

A wide variety of options are available for the delivery of your active and passive activities. Many can be integrated into an LMS or used as a stand-alone activity. The technology you choose will primarily be dependent on

Be creative with technology

the number of participants you have and the learning objectives you want them to meet. Some technology and applications are free; others will require a purchasing or subscription fee.

Below are technology ideas that may be useful for online courses. Specific brand names are not listed below due to the rapid pace of change in technology. However, if you search the terms below, you will be able to review the currently highest-rated software applications in these categories and their specific features and pricing structures.

- **Learning Suites.** Learning suites offer a cloud-based classroom that allows for document store, assignment submission, lesson delivery, activities, assessments, and collaborative workspaces.
- **Blogs or Websites.** You may wish to create a blog or website to host course material or resources. You may also ask participants to design a website or use a blog for reflection activities.
- **Collaborative and Shared Documents.** Some programs permit teams to collaborate on documents simultaneously. Groups can use these for projects to keep team members from having to email documents drafts back and forth. You can also use collaborative files for active learning exercises (see Strategy 6).
- **Writing and Drawing Programs.** You can use drawing programs to chart, take notes, or use for brainstorming and other activities.
- **Quiz or Polling Tools.** You can design a quiz or poll and provide login information to the participants. Some of these applications will generate individual or team-based competitions. Other software programs will enable you to conduct pre- and post-test (see Strategy 23) and issue certificates.
- **Video Conferencing Platforms.** You may want to use a live video to interact with the participants. Many of these platforms come with screen sharing and virtual whiteboard features.
- **Video Recording Software.** You can also use software to record yourself and your screen while narrating information. Some

programs will allow you to interject quiz questions throughout your recordings.

- **Video-Sharing Applications.** You can use a variety of applications for quick video sharing between facilitators and participants. Quickly recorded on a mobile device, sharing videos through this medium is excellent for demonstrating and assessing physical skills.
- **Animation Creators.** As an alternative to voiced-over PowerPoints, you can design animations with a voice-over narrative. You could also assign learners to create an animated project based on course content.
- **Graphic Design Programs.** Most graphic design programs permit users to a selected amount of free content. You or your participants can use these programs to design infographics, branding material, or other personalized graphics.
- **Simulation Software.** Depending on your course content, there may be a simulation software available to meet your needs. Participants usually engage in a scenario and can be evaluated based on their decision-making skills.
- **Other Software.** There are many additional types of programs that may enhance your course. Mapping or timeline software, mind-mapping or brainstorming tools, flowchart software, word cloud generators, digital portfolios, podcast software, video creation programs, meme generators, and storytelling programs are options. Be creative with technology.

Conclusion

There are countless technological options for your course delivery. You want to choose the options that will best enable you to guide your participants through the course objectives. A dynamic course includes both passive (you delivering information) and active (participate driven learning). Chose the technology that seamlessly integrates both in your class.

Apply This Strategy

- Describe the WHY of your course and calculate how many participants are usually in your class. Based on those two factors, list the platform options you can use to deliver your content and share resources, instructions, or activities.
- Review your course objectives. What is one program or application that you could use to provide content, collaborate with participants, or apply for an exercise or assessment?

Strategy 8: Transform the PowerPoints

PowerPoints are useful to guide sessions and beneficial for presenting visual information. However, many trainers use PowerPoint as the primary teaching tool. They tend to put all the words they want to say on the slide and then proceed to read word-for-word through their presentation.

Dynamic facilitators use PowerPoints as a supplement to their lectures and sessions. They are not dependent on their slides. Instead, making wise use of their slides, they enhance their presentations by providing valuable information to the learners.

A well-designed PowerPoint contains headers that describe the topic, outline key points, and present related graphics and charts. The slides are easy to read with appropriate font colors and sizes that contrast well with the background. No slides contain entire paragraphs and are full of words.

See below for additional tips for creating well-designed slides.
- Keep words to a minimum. *As a guide*, each slide should have no more than six lines and approximately ten words per bullet.
- Include a graphic, picture, or chart on most of the slides.
- Use a couple of colors but not too many. Keep the colors consistent throughout the presentation.
- Make sure the background is not overly busy.
- Ensure font colors contrast well with the background.
- Make sure fonts are not too small (nor too big).
- *In general,* keep font style and sizes consistent throughout the presentation unless highlighting specific information or data.
- Do not use much animation.
- Reduce the number of slides by using other facilitation methods, such as a virtual whiteboard, video, active learning exercise, partner discussion, or case study.

- If there is a large amount of information to share, use Word documents, Excel sheets, or web pages. Provide participants access to a shared folder or include hyperlinks in a PDF or slide.
- You can add presentation notes for yourself on the notes section rather than putting all the words on the slide.

Dynamic facilitators use PowerPoint to enhance presentations but are not dependent on the slides

---

Example of a Poorly-Designed Slides

Examples of Well-Designed

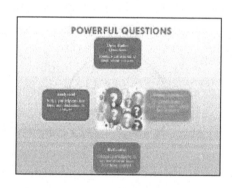

Master Facilitators

Exceptional speakers do not need much at all on their PowerPoints. Watch a few TED talks. You will notice these presenters do not rely on PowerPoints with bullets. Instead, they only use

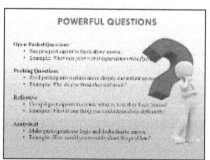

media to play a video or show a picture that illustrates a point or example. A dynamic facilitator confidently delivers the material with only a few well-chosen visual aids.

Conducting Sessions without PowerPoint

Facilitators tend to use a slide for each activity or discussion point. Often when the facilitator is using a PowerPoint, the participants are passively listening to the facilitator talk. However, there are times when it can be appropriate not to use a slide at all.

One way to reduce the need for a PowerPoint is to shift toward an active learning strategy. Look at your session and ask yourself this question: If a PowerPoint would not open on your computer, could you find a way to conduct your session? Asking this question can stimulate creative ideas to present information and help participants learn.

Take some of your slides or content and try to transition the slides from a passive lecture to an active approach. Then, determine if you need the slide at all.

> **Example A**
> Reading off a Slide (Passive Learning Approach): A slide lists ten safe operating tips with the facilitator talking through each practice.
>
> Alternative Active Learning Approach: Ask everyone to write down one idea for operational safety advice. Have a participant open a Word document on their computer and share their screen (or use a virtual whiteboard). As each participant lists their item, that participant types their answers into the Word document. See if the group can list all of the tips you planned to cover.

Example B

Reading off a Slide (Passive Learning Approach): A chart showing the reasons why employees resist change.

Alternative Active Learning Approach: Tell participants you want to discuss why employees resist change and that you are going to call on random participants. When you call on them, they are to act out an employee resisting change. The group guesses what the participant is acting out. Each participant should try to give a different example when it is their turn.

Conclusion

Presentation slides are beneficial for enhancing the visual aspect of the course. Share data or charts to illustrate valuable information but do not be dependent on reading directly from the slide. Make sure to use consistent font sizes and styles and that the font color contrasts from the background. Great facilitators can present using media only to show an example or make a point. There can be times you can direct activities or present without a PowerPoint.

Apply This Strategy

- Take one of your slides. Using the guidelines above, edit the slide to make valuable use of the visual display.
- Pretend you are doing a TED Talk on the information you are presenting. Remove all slides except for the two to three that you may need to show an object or to make a point.
- Pick a portion of your content that uses a slide. Hide the slide and see if you can find a creative way to present the information or use an active learning strategy for the content.

Strategy 9: Charting on Virtual Whiteboards

Some facilitators may be intimidated to write on virtual whiteboards because they are not artistic or do not have good handwriting. However, if you can use a virtual board while talking to the class, you can avoid using PowerPoint for some of your presentations. You can also take notes while participants are talking or conduct brainstorming activities. Some video conference programs allow you to share a virtual whiteboard. You can record as you present and send links of the recording to participants.

If you have a device with a stylus, there are other writing and drawing applications. As you fill the screen, you can scroll and continue writing. When you finish, you can save and send the file to the participants.

For recorded or live courses, you can also train your camera on a real whiteboard and use it just as if you were in an in-person classroom. Practice doodling before your session to get comfortable with the features of virtual whiteboards.

You can try some of these ideas to use while presenting:

Write a header and bullets as you talk to highlight steps or points
• Use 2-3 colors   • Use very basic drawings or symbols

Draw concept maps or mind maps as you talk

- Use several colors
- Use a bubble in the middle as a starting point
- Make boxes or squiggles around

Use virtual whiteboards for brainstorming or concept mapping activities

---

Draw storyboards or pieces of a picture or scene as you talk

- Scene take shape over the course of the session
- Use basic shapes
- Draw color-shaded boxes

Make an agenda that looks like a roadmap

- Indicate that you completed a section by highlighting, checking off, or adding details to the road map.
- Use basic symbols
- Draw color-shaded boxes

CLEAR GOALS

S
M
A
R
T

Use an acronym

- Complete an acronym throughout the presentation OR
- Have participants try to guess the word that matches the next letter based on the activity they completed
- Outline letters and fill in

Conclusion

You can use a virtual whiteboard as a visual presentation aid. You can use it for agendas or brainstorming. Write acronyms or draw a storyboard while talking. Practice doodling to get a feel for the drawing features. Using a virtual whiteboard can take the place of a PowerPoint during some sessions.

Apply This Strategy

- Open a whiteboard or memo application. Practice changing pen colors and sizes. Try writing block letters and bubble letters.
- Look at the agenda for your course. Try making a road map. Many devices will allow you to paste pictures in as well. If you are not confident with drawing, add graphics to your road map. Practice drawing a stick figure progressing on the road or checking off sections.
- Look through your PowerPoint for a process or concepts with steps. Practice discussing the steps while writing on the whiteboard. The next time you facilitate that session, try using the virtual whiteboard instead of the PowerPoint for that material.

Strategy 10: Use Social Media (Carefully)

Designing activities using social media can be a fun addition to a virtual class. With careful consideration of your participants and the learning objectives, you can leverage a variety of social media platforms to create interactive opportunities.

Be mindful of the participants in the course and their ability to navigate technology. Do not assume all participants know how to use the same applications. A survey for the pre-work will help you identify which social media your participants use regularly. Make sure all participants have downloaded the app and created a login before the session to save time.

If you use social media, dedicate part of the pre-work or beginning of the course to discuss appropriate uses of social media. Prohibit disrespectful language, graphics, or memes. Remind participants that social media posts last forever; therefore, they should use discretion in what they share. You can create professional profiles to avoid using your personal social media accounts for course interaction. Design the interactions so that participants do not have to friend or follow anyone from their personal pages if they do not desire.

Design social media activities to meet the learning objectives of the course. Identify what you want the participants to learn and create interactions to achieve those goals. You can use social media for participants to create real content for an organization. Make sure the activities you choose are not so laborious that you lose valuable course content time.

Here are some ideas for social-media-based activities:
- Have participants create a themed Facebook Page. For example, they could create a "On-the-Job Safety" page. They could post safety pictures and videos based on the content they learn in the

training sessions. They could alternatively create a business Facebook profile.

- #hashtag learned information. Set up a Twitter handle for the course. Have students tweet short quips on content or information they have learned. Summarizing activities such as this can be useful for a review or debriefing exercise.
- Set up a collaborative blog. Have participants write short blog entries as a way to recap or reflect on the information presented.
- Give participants a topic related to your content. Give them three minutes to find memes or GIFs relating to that content. If on a video conference, ask them to screen share their favorite.
- Have participants set up a Pinterest board and save pins relating to the content of the class.
- Use dance video applications for icebreakers.
- Use video recording applications for skills practice and demonstrations.
- Have participants make an Instagram story or YouTube video based on course content.
- Allow participants to use social media to reach out and interview experts.
- Have participants connect on professional networking platforms.
- Suggest participants post notable work on their Linked In or other professional networking profiles.

Social media activities can add a different element of interaction to your course

Conclusion

You can use social media appropriately for fun and real-world interactions with your participants. There are many create and apply learning activities you can implement through social media. Check that all participants are comfortable working on the platform you choose and that they use proper online etiquette when engaging with one another.

Apply This Strategy

- Which social media platform are you most comfortable with? Based on your course content, develop one activity using that platform.
- Identify the skills your participant should master by the end of your course. Give them instructions to make a YouTube video demonstrating those skills.

Part 3: Organizing the Learning

Strategy 11: Apply A Three-Phase Training Design Approach

You can maximize time outside of the course to provide additional learning opportunities. In traditional training, participants log in and complete the training session prepared by the facilitator. The participants then receive a certificate or credit for attending the course.

The learning takes place during the training session. There is no follow up to determine if the participants applied what they learned in their position. Nobody is tracking participants to assess the effectiveness of the training.

Training that has a significant impact on performance outcomes has two additional components to the actual training session: a preparation phase and an application phase. The preparation phase plays a vital role in establishing the learning process. The application phase is essential for training to make a meaningful impact on performance metrics.

The three phases in order are:
- Prepare (before the training)
- Conduct (the training time)
- Apply (after the training)

Prepare. Conduct. Apply.

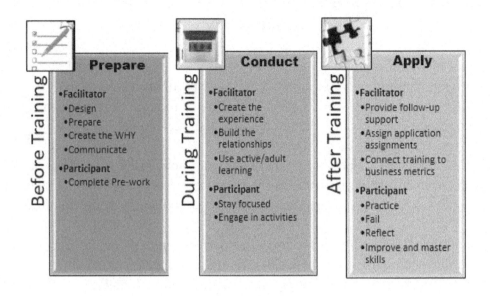

Look carefully at the figure above. There are responsibilities for the facilitator and the participant in all three phases. This guide focuses primarily on the facilitator's role. It is your responsibility to communicate to the participant that learning is active and requires work on their part also in all three phases for the training to be useful.

Subsequent chapters in this section will focus on specific information relating to these phases.

- Preparing for the training is discussed in Strategy 12.
- Conducting the training is covered in Strategies 13-21.
- Applying the training is expanded upon in Strategy 22.

Sports Analogy

A facilitator is similar to a coach. Consider the following sports analogy: A golfer shoots an average of 98 per round and would like to average 87.

Consistently shooting an 87 is the performance goal. The golfer will be working with the Pro as his coach.

Prepare: Before the Lesson

-The Pro meets with the golfer, and they discuss the goal of the golfer shooting an 87. The Pro describes the learning and practice process for the golfer to achieve that goal.

-The Pro assigns videos for the golfer to watch on the correct form.

-The Pro uses video analysis software to analyze the golfer's swing and reviews previous games. He determines the golfer's drives are good, but his pitching and putting skills are weak.

-They both agree on the time and effort it will take to achieve the goal.

Conduct: The Lesson

-The Pro coaches the golfer through a lesson on chipping and putting.

-The Pro gives the golfer practice assignments for the next two weeks.

Apply: After the Lesson

-Throughout the week, the golfer practices chipping and putting.

-The Pro follows up via phone

-The golfer plays once a week and spends an hour a day focusing on chipping and putting.

-The golfer reflects that sand traps are particularly tricky.

-A subsequent lesson concentrates only on sandtraps.

-The golfer plays in a tournament and shoots an 87.

As you can see in the analogy, the lesson itself is just one part of the entire learning process. The same principle applies to the course you design. Think of yourself as a coach. Your goal is to prepare your participants to master the course content. The training starts with preparation, continues during the lesson, and is applied later in the work setting.

Conclusion

The training session is just one of three phases for a successful learning process. Communicating with the participants ahead of time allows you to set goals, introduce yourself, and answer questions. The training session includes the content you deliver and the activities you facilitate. The third phase is following through with the attendee by providing support and additional materials for their success.

Apply this Strategy

- Think of a recent course you attended or facilitated. Did it have a Three-Stage Training Approach? If it did, what activities did you complete before and after the training? If it did not use this approach, what would be some pre- and post-activities you would recommend for that trainer to use?
- Review the graphic on the previous page. Circle what is currently completed by you (the facilitator) and the participants in your current training style. Which additional phases could you add to enhance your course?

Strategy 12: Have the Participants Prepare

The preparation phase occurs before the actual training session takes place. A well-designed preparation phase permits you to maximize the time in your course. Having the participants prepare for a learning event enhances their knowledge acquisition and skill acquisition.

The goals of the pre-session activities are to:
1. Build connections between participants and facilitators
2. Initiate relationships between the group of participants
3. Reduce participants' anxiety
4. Provide context or materials to set a foundation for the session
5. Introduce the WHY—Help participants understand why the training is important

Here are ideas to meet the Preparation Phase goals:
- Record a voiced-over PowerPoint or video introducing yourself. Include relevant pictures of yourself, your job, role in the company, educational settings, work experience, family, or hobbies. Including some personal information about yourself will help you seem more approachable to the participants.
- If working with a small group, call or have a short video conference with the participants individually or as a group. Introduce yourselves. Ask them to discuss their goals for the training. Pre-communication can also be a time for participants to check sound and video connections.
- Send an email that includes clear, concise information for the course. Include URL link, username reminders, or password information. Be as specific as possible. Remember, some participants may not be technologically savvy—even younger participants—so do not assume they know how to navigate the technology you are using. The email can include the course agenda, break times, and learning objectives. If you are going to

have the participants complete post-work to apply session content, indicate the type and scope of activities they will complete, so they are clear on the overall time commitment of the training.

- Email a tutorial video on how to use any features of the LMS or applications you will be using during the training. Keep this video pinned or readily accessible in case participants need to refer to it during the session.

- Include a short video of a senior leader introducing your course and explaining how the content is vital to the organization. Their message helps create the WHY and helps participants see the value in spending the time in the session.

A well-designed preparation phase maximizes your time in class

---

- Depending on the size of the class, ask participants to post a one-minute video introducing themselves. You can also ask them to answer one fun question (e.g., their favorite ice cream flavor) or a question related to the content of the course (e.g., their worse customer experience in a customer relation course). Review the videos and prepare a "Who Is It?" document. Email the participants questions, such as "Which course participant had a customer come around and try to use the register themselves?" Which course participant had a customer that intentionally broke glass items in the grocery store?" Have the participants watch the videos to answer the questions. This icebreaker is an excellent way for participants to get to know each other and may provide you with real-world examples to use in your training session. To modify this for a larger-sized course, use a polling application to ask the question. You can read through some of the answers at the beginning of the video conference.

- Consider sending paperwork or a learning module ahead of time to enhance learning. Participants can learn concepts individually. The training module can include more remembering and understanding objectives. You will then be able to spend more time in the training session for application or creating learning objectives (see Strategy 1). Make sure the pre-work is not too extensive and is directly related to the learning outcomes for the training.
- If you are going to use a software or application where the participants need to create a login, send a link before the course, and encourage everyone to login ahead of time.
- Use pre-work to build excitement using techniques to hook the audience. Create curiosity and value for the time the participant will spend in the course, which is vital since people want to know the training is worth attending (see Strategy 5).
- Create short review documents or videos. This material should be content you expect everyone in the course to know before joining the session. Tell the participants you will begin the training with a short quiz on that material to encourage them to review the concepts.

Conclusion

There are vital things you must communicate before your class starts: the course expectations and the value of the course. The pre-course work is a great time to introduce yourself and start learning about the participants. You can use a quiz or poll to review material or determine the participants' learning styles. Small teasers or object lessons are great methods to build excitement for your course.

- In the context of your specific training and course delivery methods, how could you introduce yourself to the participants before the training starts?
- What concepts might be review material or easy to communicate with a pre-work assignment?

Strategy 13: Open with a Bang

The opening activities of a session can make or break a training event. The very first activities should accomplish two goals:
1. Capture the participants' attention
2. Get participants to interact

Facilitators often *start* the training with the course agenda and learning objectives. These items are essential. However, spending time to capture the participants' attention and have them interact sets the stage for increased participation in active learning activities and produces effective results.

If you can pique the curiosity of your participants at the beginning of a session, it will increase their willingness to participate in the learning process. It also increases energy during active learning segments and discussions. The interaction helps build relationships and eases tension, which improves participation. Increased participation leads to better learning outcomes. Only *after* you have their attention and have jumpstarted participant interaction should you explain the why of the course and the learning objectives.

Capture Their Attention

Below are some ideas to grab their attention. The activities can be used at the very beginning of the course and used to begin individual sessions.
- Tell the start of a compelling story but leave the group hanging for the ending, which you reveal within the session. In an asynchronous course, start the story in a video at the beginning of the module. Tell the class that the ending of the story is embedded further along in the module.
- In the room where you are recording or via screen share or slides, show objects that connect to a subject. You can have participants

take guesses as to the connection of the items, then tell them they will find out later in the session.

- Have raffle items connect to your content and show them off at the beginning. Tell the participants you will raffle them off at different times during the session or as rewards for participating in activities.
- Make a short quiz or survey with questions about the content that do not have obvious answers. Use a response feature that allows the group to see the number of responses for each answer option. Tell the participants you will give them the correct answers during the sessions.
- Pretend you are a newscaster or podcaster. Pretend you are on air. Introduce yourself and provide a teaser at the beginning of a module. If you are creative, add a jingle. Every time you end a session, give a teaser for the next segment or class. An adaptation for an asynchronous course is to use short recorded videos.
- Play a brief television, movie, song, or advertisement clip related to your content. Tell the participants that the clip connects to the session content and that you will tie it in later. As you begin talking, the participants will be thinking about how the clip is relating to what you are sharing.
- Show participants a quote or phrase with several words missing that has a link to your content. Tell them to try to figure out the missing words by the end of the session. If you teach an asynchronous course, embed the missing words into your modules. The participants can "hunt" for the missing words as they go through the course.

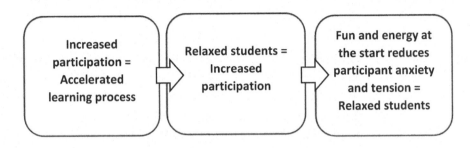

Get Participants to Interact

- Tell the group they are not allowed to talk for the first five minutes. Instead, they have to use the chat feature of the video conferencing tool to introduce themselves. Tell them the goal is to find two other participants who have similar interests. You can start the chat to get it rolling and then let them go.
- Ask the participants to choose a virtual background that is mostly one of the three primary colors (red, blue, or green). Once they have chosen backgrounds, give them different discussion prompts based on their background color (e.g., everyone who has a red background has to share what excites them about the course).
- Instruct participants to introduce themselves and then in charade-style, act out their favorite hobby while the other participants guess the hobby. If on a phone call, participants have to describe the hobby without using its name while others guess. For an asynchronous class, have students upload a short video introducing themselves while doing their hobby. For example, if someone likes to bake, have them do their introduction video while baking (or pretending to bake).
- Assign participants to create a logo and tagline for themselves in pre-course communication. During the session, allow them to screen share and explain what they designed.

- Introduce yourself and share something you hate that everyone else likes (or pick any other question for the participants to answer). Then randomly choose the name of a participant. They have to introduce themselves and answer the questions. Then they get to select the name of the next participant to answer the question.
- Play Scattergories. Make a Scattegories list of 8-12 items that may be related to the topic area of your training (or google to find a fun list). Roll an alphabet dice or use a random letter generator to pick a letter. Give everyone two minutes to fill out the list based on the letter. Go through each item and allow people to share what they wrote.
- Play bingo with words or ideas that connect to the topic of your content.
- In the pre-session communication, ask participants to join the session with an item (real or a picture) that explains their work style (or give them a prompt specific to your content). Ask each participant to introduce themselves and explain their item. For a large group, provide the participants three to five pictures. Ask them to choose which image best describes their personality (or use another prompt) using a polling application. Show the first item and ask a few of the people who selected that item to introduce themselves. Continue for the rest of the pictures.

Pique the participants' curiosity at the beginning of a session

---

Get Participants to Interact—Ideas Specific to Asynchronous Courses

If you are teaching an asynchronous course, here are ideas using shared documents or discussion boards. It is preferable to use a discussion forum where all replies are easily viewable. Forums without easily visible responses are not conducive to foster engaging interactions. If you use a shared document, you may be able to put the discussion prompts into the background (so that the participants do not delete them) and add text boxes where the participants should type. All of these ideas can also be used as pre-work or adapted for synchronous sessions.

- Create a shared "Introduce Yourself" document. Make three columns labeled: Name, Picture, About You, and Replies. Have the participants fill out the information about themselves in the first three columns. In the last column, instruct participants to leave comments to their colleagues.
- Play "Who Has Done the Following?" Or "My Favorites" or some other list relating to your training content. Post a shared document with a list of questions (who has worked at one company for more than ten years? Who has been part of a Skype interview?). Have participants read the list and add their name next to the appropriate items in the list.
- Have the participants watch a short video clip that has multiple characters (The Office, Parks and Recreation, or the Mickey Mouse Show). Make a shared document that has a picture and title for each character (e.g., you might title Jim Halpert from The Office "The Office Jokester"). Instruct each participant to put their name and post a picture next to the character with whom they best identify. They can add a short sentence or two to explain why they are like that character.
- Present a teaser related to your topic in your session. In a shared document, post face emojis that could be used to describe the topic. Ask the participants to put their name and picture next to the emoji that best describes how they feel about the topic. If you are using a discussion forum, ask the participants to use emojis of their choice that describe how they feel about the topic.

Conclusion

Open with a bang to create excitement and generate energy in the course. Use a teaser or hook to pique the participants' interest. Complete an activity for the participants to interact. The activity at the beginning of the course will foster an environment conducive for stimulating discussions and enthusiastic, active learning.

Apply This Strategy

- Think of your favorite podcast or newscaster. What do they do well to hook you into their podcast or video? How can you replicate this for your session?
- Put a star by the interaction idea that you think would energize your participants the most.

Strategy 14: Establish the Why

Once you have gotten your participants' attention and had them interact, you have **one more critical task** to accomplish before you share the agenda and learning objectives to have a dynamic session.

You need to establish the **WHY**. The participants must know WHY they need the content of the course. They need to realize the value of mastering the learning objectives. You want to get the participants' buy-in from the very beginning for an optimal learning environment.

The way you can establish the value is to refer back to the reason the course was designed (see Strategy 1). Why was this training course implemented? Why will this training matter to the day-to-day operations of the company? Why does senior management think they need to invest in this training? Make the examples and reasoning specific to the attendees.

Only then should you introduce WHAT the participants will learn (the learning objectives) and HOW they will do it (the agenda).

To open your course, use the order below:
- WHY (the value) for the participant
- WHAT (learning objectives) the participants will do
- HOW the participants will accomplish the learning objectives (course agenda)

Keeping this order in mind will help you create a dynamic opening for your training course.

Why (The Value)

From the very beginning, you want the attendees to see the value of the course for their position, unit, or career. If the participants do not understand the significance of learning your material or think it is merely busywork, they will not invest in the learning process.

It does not take much time to justify value. Go back to WHY the course was created and find a meaningful way to communicate it to the participants. If possible, personalize the WHY to the specific group of attendees. For example, if you have a safety training course, you might want to provide a different rationale for the chemical processing unit than you would for the food safety unit.

To establish the WHY, you can use stories or testimonials, or conduct a short activity that highlights a problem or need and how your course will provide a solution.

Here are some examples:

- If you are talking about overcoming fear of presenting, you could open with this story:

  We had a participant recently who absolutely could not stand in front of a group. Today, she is in a full-time training role traveling to other locations and has no fear. What did she learn to make such a drastic turnaround? In our first module today, we will share what she learned.

- If you were conducting a session for new frontline leaders, you could start with this story:

During the last year, we promoted two new supervisors.
One was very successful in engaging their team while the
other one struggled and could not gain credibility. There
were three differences between the two. In our session
today, we will provide you with the factors the successful
one used, so you can apply them to your leadership
approach.

- Have participants explain a problem in their area that needs to be solved. If you were doing a class on time management, have the participants call out frustrations they face at work. List a few illustrations from each group on a virtual whiteboard. You will see a connection between their examples and your content. Explain how the topics covered will address many of these issues.

The participants must recognize the value of the time
they invest in your course

What

This step involves you explaining WHAT the participants will do in your course (see Strategy 1). You will describe the learning objectives they will master when they finish. In a sense, you are explaining WHAT they will walk away with by the end of the process.

Three to six learning objectives is a reasonable amount of goals for a training course. You can assign a learning objective to a session and then break it down into smaller learning tasks.

Here are some creative ideas to present the learning objectives instead of just reading them:

71

- Post a slide of the objectives and let the participants observe them for a minute. Ask them for words that stand out to them. Use the words to help them get a deeper understanding of the goal.
- Have an object in the room that relates to a learning objective. Tell the participants when you get to that learning objective, you will explain the item's meaning (see Strategy 5).
- Ask the participants to look at the objectives and share which one they think will help them the most. If several participants share and there are learning objectives that they have not mentioned, explain that objective more and ask how accomplishing it will help them.
- Generate a word cloud using your learning objectives. Ask the participants what words stick out to them.
- Show participants the list of learning objectives and ask them which one(s) look the most interesting to them.

How (Agenda):

This part shows the participants HOW they will learn the objectives. The HOW includes the agenda or roadmap. It gives them a sense of direction and what to expect during the day.

The HOW also includes an overview of how you plan to run the course. You can share that your sessions are interactive and incorporate active learning strategies. You can introduce them to the types of learning methods you use, such as PowerPoints, videos, case studies, and activities. If you are going to use applications or less-commonly used features of your LMS, briefly show them how to use the elements and ensure they know how to locate troubleshooting instructions.
You can also include information about breaks. Some facilitators will review a code of conduct or ground rules. You may also want to discuss guidelines on respectful virtual engagement.

Asking participants for their expectations is another potential activity during this time. Ideally, they understand the scope of the course already so that they are not surprised. If a person states an expectation that you do not plan to cover, let them know.

Conclusion

Always address the why before the how. Before going into the course content, make sure the participants understand the worth of the course. Examples and case studies are useful for demonstrating value. The participants then need to know what they are trying to accomplish. You should only explain the how, or the instruction, after that.

Apply This Strategy

- What is the value of your course? What is the best way to help a participant quickly see this value for themselves?
- Have you attended a course that presented the why, what, or how creatively? How could you modify that method for your session?

Strategy 15: Organize The Learning Process in Groups of Threes

As the course facilitator, your role is to organize the learning process. An excellent course is methodically planned and helps your participants to understand the course objectives and content clearly. The material is presented in a logical sequence and with clear connections linking the information presented.

You can use these three groups of "threes" to structure your course:
- Courses, Session, and Activities
- Opening, Content, and Close
- Why, What, and How

Course, Sessions, and Activities

The entire course is your starting point. To narrow the focus of the course, ask yourself: What are the overarching goals and objectives of the whole course? For some courses, the objectives will be few and easy to master and may only need to be an hour long. Other courses may have multiple learning objectives or involve skills that the participants will need time to practice.

Courses with this level of complexity may last several days or a week. The length of your class should be dependent on the amount of time it will take for the participants to complete the learning objectives (see Strategy 20).

Divide the course into sessions. The course objectives determine the number of sessions. Some courses may have one session; others may have multiple sessions over several days. For asynchronous courses, you might call these sessions "modules."

Within a session, there should be both active learning exercises and passive learning information delivery. All learning activities should be directly related to the session's learning outcomes.

Therefore, you should have
1. The entire course, broken into
2. Sessions (or modules), comprised of
3. Individual learning activities

Opening, Content, Close

Next, consider the components of the course, sessions, and activities. For each of these, you are going to have three parts: An opening, the content, and the close.

The opening is a quick activity that introduces the content, demonstrates the value of the material, captures the participants' attention, and explains the objectives. The content is composed of content delivery and learning exercises. Ideally, a mix of active and passive exercises are employed (see Strategy 18). The close is a debrief of the content and acts as the conclusion. The debrief can include a wrap-up activity, reflection, or review exercise. The course, each session, and every activity should contain an opening, content, and close.

Your training **course** should have three parts:
1. The Opening
2. The Content
3. The Close

If you are conducting a full day course with four sessions, the opening occurs first in the morning. You may choose to start with an icebreaker, an energetic "bang" activity (see Strategy 13), and the course agenda. The remaining sessions are then the "content" of the course. At the end of the workshop, the last activity will be your "close." You may choose to do a 3-2-1 exercise (three things you learned, two concepts you will apply, one question you still have) or other reflection activity (see Strategy 17).

Individual modules or sessions should have the same sequence:
1. The Opening
2. The Content
3. The Close

Imagine you have four sessions in your course. At the beginning of each session, start with an opening. This opening might be an object lesson, story, challenge, or activity designed to introduced the topic and objectives of that specific session. Then, you will guide the participants through the active and passive learning exercises you planned for that session. That would be considered the session's content. At the end of the session, you will provide a closing comprised of a skills demonstration, a virtual "snowball" quiz (each participant gets to choose the next participant to answer a question), or review activity.

All activities within a module or session should follow the pattern as well.
1. The Opening
2. The Content
3. The Close

Each activity should begin with an opening. More specific details about how to open an activity are below. The participants should then complete the exercise. Before moving to the next activity in the session, there should be a conclusion or debriefing period. Facilitators often jump from activity to activity without explaining how all of the exercises relate to the overall course objectives. Close the first activity before shifting to the next task. Provide smooth transitions between activities and clear connections between the tasks the participants complete and the course objectives.

Why, What, and How

There is one additional sequence of three that you are going to add to this concept. Each opening, content, and close should have a How, What, and Why.

Strategy 1 introduced three essential questions when designing the course: Why (value), What (objectives), and How (instructions). Embed these three questions into every opening, content, and close sequence.

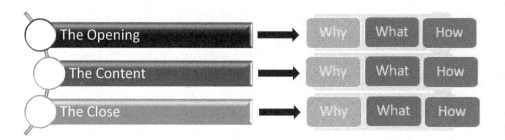

Many facilitators rush straight to the how—the agenda or instructions—without explaining the why and the what. Initially describing the why, what, and how in every aspect of the course will seem excessive. However, once you understand and practice this concept, you will be able to deliver the information seamlessly, and the participants will not recognize what you are doing. This delivery method will keep participants engaged and increase their learning capacity.

Why, What, and How for Activities:

The way a facilitator opens, executes, and closes an exercise can make or break its usefulness. Often, a facilitator will say something similar to this: "Now we are going to do an exercise." Or "We are going to watch a little video and then talk about it."

Participants want to know WHY they are doing each activity in a workshop and how it connects to the learning objectives. If you tell them to chart, watch a video, or practice a skill without context, they may be confused, anxious, or lack motivation.

Using Why, What, and How, you provide the *context* for the activity and build *value* for the participants. Many facilitators explain the HOW first by going straight to the activity instructions. However, it is crucial to explain the **WHY first** to create the value. Then the WHAT or final output, and finally, HOW to get to the result.

Here is an example:

> **Go from Saying This:** We are going to list the reasons we face resistance from our employees. **To:**

> Why As leaders, we have all faced resistance from employees at some point. There are three practical approaches we can incorporate as leaders to reduce this resistance.

> What Let's create a list of the types of resistance you face. Then we will discuss how to use these three approaches to address those challenges.

> How I'm going to open a virtual whiteboard. Call out examples of resistance you have faced, and I will write your responses. When we have our list, I will show you three approaches to minimize resistance and match them to your specific challenge.

Example 2: Go from Saying This: "Please watch this video." **To:**

Why   In our pre-work assignment, you all mentioned that it is hard not to use filler words, such as um, you know, ahh. That is one of the biggest challenges for any speaker or facilitator.

What   There are many ways to address this issue, but there are three specific things you can do to reduce these filler words by 80% immediately.

How   Watch this two-minute video clip and identify the three things this speaker does to eliminate most of the filler words. I have the three items listed under this chart. We will see if you can discover them first. Giving clear instructions for activities can be difficult. One way to implement this concept is to create a slide with Why, What, and How prompts. This format will help you visualize the right order and provide full instructions to your participants.

Explain the why, what, and how throughout the entire course

The following graphic is a model demonstrating a training course that has two sessions. The model indicates how to use open, content, and close throughout each part. It also shows that the why, what, and how are part of each aspect as well.

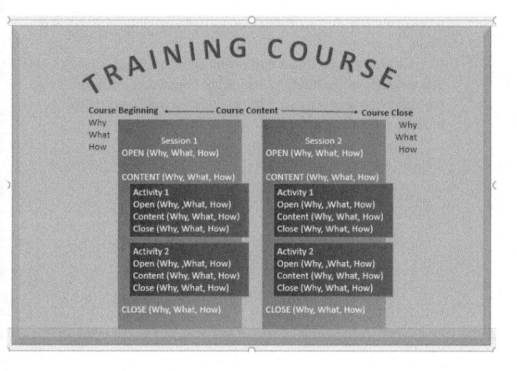

TRAINING COURSE

Course Beginning ←————— Course Content —————→ Course Close

Why
What
How

Session 1	Session 2
OPEN (Why, What, How)	OPEN (Why, What, How)
CONTENT (Why, What, How)	CONTENT (Why, What, How)
Activity 1 Open (Why, ,What, How) Content (Why, What, How) Close (Why, What, How)	**Activity 1** Open (Why, ,What, How) Content (Why, What, How) Close (Why, What, How)
Activity 2 Open (Why, ,What, How) Content (Why, What, How) Close (Why, What, How)	**Activity 2** Open (Why, ,What, How) Content (Why, What, How) Close (Why, What, How)
CLOSE (Why, What, How)	CLOSE (Why, What, How)

Why
What
How

Conclusion

Use groups of threes to structure your course. The entire course is composed of sessions. Within a session, there are several activities. The course, sessions, and activities should all contain openings, content, and closing. Each component of the course includes a why, what, and how. If the delivery is smooth, the participants will not notice the repetition as you guide them through the course.

Apply This Strategy

- Look at the outline for each session or module in your course. Is there a specific opening activity that explains its value? Do you have a debriefing or review activity at the end? Do you clearly link the session to the overall course objective? What do you need to add to your sessions to ensure you have an opening, content, and close?

- Review how you facilitate the current activities in your course. Do you clearly explain the Why and What (value and learning objectives) *before* providing the instructions? What can you modify to emphasize the Why and What first?

Strategy 16: Diversify Types of Activities

As you design your course, you want to incorporate a variety of active and passive facilitation methods. Diversifying activities will help the students stay engaged.

However, you do not want to implement an assortment of activities just to make the course enjoyable. Instead, dynamic facilitators strategically choose the presentation and learning activities based on the course goal and objectives.

First, consider the **WHY** of the training course. Why does the business want to invest in this course? Why does this course bring value to the company?

Then consider the **WHAT** of the training course. What are the intended learning objectives?

From there, create the **HOW**. Deliberately choose the most advantageous learning strategies combinations that will guide the participant to master the learning objectives.

As you design your course, you want to use both active and passive learning activities. Strategy 6 outlines many specific learning activities organized by Bloom's Taxonomy. Active learning exercises conducted in a virtual setting can include recall, understanding, application, analytical, evaluation, and creating exercises. One bullet point in the following chart refers to all of the examples in that strategy.

Below is a general list of passive and active facilitation methods you can use for your course.

Vary the activities to keep the participants engaged. Strategically choose the array of activities based on the intended learning outcomes of the course.

Passive Activities	Active Learning Exercises	Other
• Ice Breakers (Strategy 13) • Stories (Strategy 13) • Videos • TV Clips • Charting Exercises (Strategy 9) • Show Pre-recorded Interviews • Object Lessons • Ask Questions	• Case Studies • Brainstorming (use virtual whiteboard) • Games • Experiential Activities (record experiences) • Role Play (use video features) • Fill-In PDF Worksheets • Small-Group Discussions (use video chat breakout room) • Active Learning Exercises (Strategy 6) • Reflections	• Pre-Work (Strategy 12) • Icebreakers (Strategy 13) • Competitions • Assessments • Social Media (Strategy 10) • Post-Work (Strategy 22)

How many activities do you need for your course? As many as you need for your participants to master the learning objectives.

Which activities are the most effective? It will depend on your specific course. As a dynamic facilitator, it is your job to carefully consider how you can best help your participants meet the course outcomes.

Strategically choose a diverse array of activities based on the intended learning objectives of the course

---

Conclusion

Keep your course from being boring. Implement a variety of exercises in your class. Choose several activities that align with the courses' learning objectives. Use a mixture of active and passive learning strategies as you guide your participants. Passive activities include listening and watching. Active learning includes discussion and practice. Add as many activities to your course as needed for the participants to meet the learning outcomes.

Apply This Strategy

- Complete this brainstorming activity. In the center of a piece of paper, draw a circle. Inside, write down the WHY of your course. Like spokes, draw lines spreading out from the circle. At the end of each line, draw a rectangle. In each rectangle, write down one of the course objectives. Radiating from each rectangle, draw 2-4 short lines. At the end of each line, write down an activity you could use to meet that learning objective.

Strategy 17: Debrief Activities

The close of a course, session, or activity should contain a specific conclusion called a debrief. The purpose of the debrief is to make sure the participants understood the specific intent (why) from the activity. The participants must understand and connect the why of the activity or session to their particular work situation. Facilitators often finish activities and transition immediately to the next exercise. While the connection between the activity and the learning objective may be evident to the facilitator, not all participants may make the association. The debriefing sessions helps to connect the dots.

The debrief may contain a review, an analysis, or a personalized application. With an effective debrief, 90% of the explanations come from the participants. Get the group to provide the key learning points from the activity instead of telling them what they should have seen or heard. The facilitator's role is to fill in missing information or clarify misconceptions.

Effective Debrief Guidelines
- Avoid filling in the missing information too quickly. Give participants time to think and ask the right probing questions.
- If you see confusion and or that participants have missed the main point, the activity may not be a good fit or the instructions may not be clear.
- If the exercise requires significant energy and thinking, allow small groups to work together and then share their insights. A case study is one example of a challenging exercise that requires a deeper level of critical thinking.
- Ensure you explain the why, what, and how of the debrief activity.

Debrief Ideas

You can conduct the following ideas as a discussion in a video chat. Participants can also write down answers on a virtual whiteboard and screen share. Facilitators can email fillable PDFs or ask participants to write down their answers on a piece of paper before the discussion. For asynchronous courses, participants can type their reflections into fillable PDFs or in a journal, blog, or discussion submissions. They can also record their answers via video.

- Ask the participants to give an example of how they will use the information in their specific work position.
- If the activity involved a role-play or decision-making, ask the participants what could have been different. If you are teaching an asynchronous course, participants can upload videos of their role-play, and write a reflection of what they could have done differently.
- Ask participants to complete a 3-2-1 assignment: Write down three things they learned, two things they will try to apply in their position, and one question they still have.
- Ask participants to list or share their "AHA" moments during the activity or session.
- Complete a Circle, Square, Triangle activity.[16] The participants answer these questions:
  - o Circle: What is still going around in your head? What do you still not understand?
  - o Squared: What is squared away? What do you genuinely understand?
  - o Triangle: What are three takeaways that you can apply to your job position?
- Ask: "What is the one thing I learned that I can start doing now and could have a big impact on my contribution?"[17]
- Ask: What ideas could be put into practice right away? If there are ideas that cannot be applied, ask why and what barriers are there.

> *The debrief may contain a review, an analysis, or a personalized application*

- Have participants quiz each other with open-ended questions.
- Draw a Tree of Knowledge. Give participants a worksheet with a tree-branch drawn on it. Ask the participants to draw on their tree with a green stylus or green marker. For the "branches," ask them to write out what they have learned.
- Develop SMART Goals. Ask the participant to choose a
  o Specific Goal
  o Measurable Goal
  o Achievable
  o Realistic
  o Timeline for the Goal
- Keeping TABBS.[17] Ask them for their **T**akeaway from the event; **A**ction they will take; **B**arriers they may face; **B**enefits to overcoming the barriers to implement the learning.
- Play Gestures: Have participants act out one action item they plan to apply based on the content of the session or activity. This game can be done live in a video chat or with the use of recorded video in an asynchronous course.

Conclusion

Use the debrief period to make sure the participants understood the purpose of the activity or session. This period is a good time to ask the participants to reflect. Make sure each participant knows how to apply the activity objective to their work setting.

Apply This Strategy

- Put a star by the two debriefing activities that you would like to add to your next course
- Describe a barrier you face when implementing debriefing activities. What solutions might help you overcome that barrier?

Strategy 18: Maintain a 40/60 Facilitation Balance

Many training sessions consist mostly of presentations delivered with the aid of a PowerPoint. People have short attention spans. During lectures, participants' attention starts to drift within ten to twelve minutes.[18] Researchers who postulate listeners can focus longer than twelve minutes still concede that presenters must be skilled at keeping their audience's attention.[19] A dynamic facilitator keeps the participants focused so they can learn as much as possible.

Switching from using primarily passive learning to using a combination of passive and active learning strategies enhances the learning process for your participants by keeping them engaged.[20]

Aiming for a 40/60 passive-to-active learning strategy ratio is a good goal. For comparison, lectures are closer to a 90/10 passive-to-active learning ratio.

Why Shift the Balance Toward More Active Learning?
- Participants have a longer attention span
- Participants are not as bored
- Participants have a higher completion rate of online modules
- Participants demonstrate higher scores on assessments
- Participants show improvement with recall and mastery
- Participants arriving with higher levels of knowledge engage with the material instead of checking out

Practical Implementation Ideas
- Do not think of active learning as busywork. Think about the WHAT of the session. What are the participants to learn by the time you finished delivering that content? Review Strategy 6 for

91

active learning in a virtual environment. Choose learning activities that correlate with the session objectives.

- Think of passive learning as "pushing" information and active learning as "pulling" information. Create a "push/pull" rhythm as you develop your sessions.
- Embed multiple-choice, true/false, case study, or other quiz questions every few minutes in a course with a pre-recorded lecture. These questions can be a useful interactive tool to maintain participants' attention through longer videos.[9]
- Use active learning strategies for review material at the beginning of a session. It is an excellent way to get participants to interact and avoid checking out while you present content they may already know.

Aim for a 40/60 passive-to-active learning strategy ratio

Determine what concepts the participants can learn by themselves through discussion, research, or an activity. Instead of lecturing on that material, let the students do the work. Correct any misconceptions or add information they missed. Save the lecture for the content they would have a difficult time learning or gathering themselves.

Example

Here is an example of a passive-active learning sequence:
- Investigation activity where participants identify the problem themselves
- Facilitator lectures with quiz questions interspersed
- Participants complete an analytical activity or practice to master a skill

- The facilitator provides additional in-depth information
- Participants complete a case study, evaluation, or creative learning exercise
- Facilitator conducts a debriefing to end session or unit

The above is just one possible way to move back and forth between passive and active learning strategies as you help your participants move from foundational to mastery concepts. The actual sequence you choose for each session will ultimately depend on your learning objectives.

Conclusion

A dynamic session includes an interchange between active and passive activities. Both are valuable for the learning process. While it can be easy to default into a passive information delivery in an online setting, it is not difficult to add in active learning.

Apply This Strategy

- Review a session from your current training course. What is the passive-to-active learning ratio in that session?
- Look through your course. Currently, what is your lengthiest lecture? How can you break up the speech with either an activity or a poll or quiz questions?
- Write down one thing you could do to shift your course to a 40/60 passive-to-active learning ratio.

Strategy 19: Plan Activities in Twenty-Minute Segments

As you develop the interactive rhythm of your sessions, plan activities in twenty-minute segments.

Planning in blocks provides a framework for you to organize your content and estimate session timing. Implementing a session with multiple activities can get complicated. Failing to structure the timing of your course can lead to some learning activities taking a long time and potentially short-changing the time you can allot to other significant information.

For example, a lengthy review may cause you to rush through an application activity at the end of the session. You may lose the participants' attention if an exercise runs too long. Conversely, if sections are too short, there is a risk of not being able to cover enough content to achieve the learning objective.

Structure your time by planning in twenty-minute blocks. Consider the learning objectives for the session. Decide what material you will deliver passively and what is appropriate for an active learning exercise. As a general rule, you want to schedule less time for remembering and understand activities and more time for application, analytical, or creative activities. Start planning the course in the twenty minute segments.

Like the 40/60 active-to-passive learning ratio, twenty-minute blocks are an approximation, not a hard and fast rule. Do not lock yourself into the twenty-minute blocks; use that time reference as a guide.

Plan content in 20-minute segments

Strategy 24 contains a sample session. In the example, you can visualize how to structure training in twenty-minute segments. Use this concept to plan your course. One-hour webinars would only need three twenty-minute blocks. If you have a full-day or multi-day class, you will have to plan how you structure each session. You can structure asynchronous training similarly.

Instead of pre-loading the modules with passive activities (lecture, reading, or videos) and then assigning activities at the end, think about the "push/pull" rhythm. Plan twenty-minute blocks. Present information and then assign a quiz or exercise so that students immediately engage the material.

Conclusion

A twenty-minute segment gives you a building block for your course. Use it as a guide to structure course activities. This guide will help you plan your timing and control the flow of information.

Apply This Strategy

- Recall a training course you attended recently. Did the facilitator present in segments? If not, what suggestions would you have for the facilitator to increase participant engagement?
- Rate yourself on a scale of 1-10 (1 = poor; 10 = excellent) of how well you stay on schedule while facilitating activities? Reflect: Do you feel you have too many activities? Or not enough activities? How would planning in twenty-minute blocks help you manage time better during sessions?

Strategy 20: Hit the Sweet Spot

How much time is the right amount of time for your training? Does it need to be one hour, or a full-day, or multiple days?

To determine HOW long the course should be, look at the answer to the WHY and WHAT course questions.

- WHY are you conducting the training? What is the end business goal of the training?
- WHAT learning objectives do you hope the participants meet by the end of your training?

You want to create training sessions that are balanced and provide enough time for the learning but not so much time that the participants lose their focus.

Hitting the Sweet Spot Analogy

Imagine training is like a perfectly ripe banana. You do not want green bananas. You do not wish to have overly ripe bananas. You want perfectly ripe, sweet bananas.

The same is true for training. You do not want to force too much material into a short period leaving participants unable to master the material. Likewise, you do not want to spend excessive time on a topic covering unnecessary material while failing to link content to outcomes.

Your goal is to provide the right mix of learning activities that help the participants master the course objectives. You want to ensure there is enough time for them to process and apply the information.

- **Material is covered too fast**
- **Not enough practice to absorb it**
- **Not clear on the purpose**

- **Right mix of learning activities**
- **Enough time to process and apply**
- **Appropriate follow-up support to master the intent**

- **Too much time on the topic**
- **Covering unneeded content**
- **No connect to the outcomes or application**

Case Example 1

A trainer had developed a one-hour webinar on battery disposal. Regular webinars were at least one hour, so he created enough slides for that length of time. He was encouraged to review his objectives and audience. The trainer determined he did not need that level of detail for this topic. He reduced the training to 20 minutes and combined it with other safety training for that group.

Lesson: Do not feel the need to prepare your training any "standard" length of time. Choose the amount of time you need based on the training objectives.

Case Example 2

A trainer usually had a several-hour time allotment to teach operators how to assemble a piece of equipment. The trainer considered the objectives of his training. He created a one-page guide to teach experienced operators how to complete the assembly tasks. Using video conference, he let the operators practice the assembly while he was on hand virtually to answer questions.

Lesson: Your training does not need to be in a standard format. Choose training activities based on your intended outcomes.

Use the course objectives to determine training session length

---

Case Example 3

A trainer conducted a half-day seminar to teach newly promoted middle managers operational and supervisory competencies. She rushed through PowerPoints and often had to cut off questions at the end. After the training, she usually received many questions regarding content she had gone over in the sessions. She reviewed the goals and the learning outcomes expected of the training and determined she was presenting too much information at once. She broke up the competencies and ran one half-day seminar each month. She used active learning techniques and post-work. The managers felt more prepared and supported in their new roles.

Lesson: Trying to force too much information into one seminar may result in participants learning very little information.

Case Example 4

At the end of every year, a senior leader ran a full-day virtual meeting. It appeared to many of the attendees that the sessions were arbitrary, pointless, and there to fill time. The leader thought about the goal of the meeting and brainstormed a way to communicate it with the attendees. She started explaining the why, what, and how of each activity. The participants began to see the value in the meetings.

Lesson: Training with little or no connection to a goal seems to lack purpose.

Conclusion

Determine the length of your course by deciding how long it will take your participants to master the course objectives. A class that is too short will result in attendees rushing through the material and not learning the content well. A long class may leave participants bored and resisting busywork. Try to find the "sweet spot" of a course just long enough to meet the intended outcomes.

Apply This Strategy

- The next time you plan a training session, evaluate the why and what, then determine your HOW. Based on how you plan to meet the learning objectives, calculate how much time is necessary for the training.
- Evaluate one of your sessions. Reviewing your goal, design with three completely different creative training plans to meet that goal. Chose one to implement.

Strategy 21: Close Strong

"Well, that is all I have for today. Thank you all for participating and have a nice day." That is how many sessions end, which may leave the participants hanging or confused. Asynchronous courses may stop at the last module and never discuss how all the modules in the course relate to each other.

A dynamic facilitator will create a purposeful and impactful ending by reviewing course objectives, clearing up misconceptions, demonstrating the relationships between course content, or providing suggestions on how to apply the material. A compelling finish to a course is similar to a captivating conclusion at the end of a book.

Ideas to create a powerful close:
- Ask participants to review the initial learning objectives or outcomes. Ask them to share one thing they learned and connect it to a course objective. If you have an asynchronous course, list the learning objectives on a shared document or forum. Ask the participants to write one thing they learned or stuck out to them for each objective.
- Ask participants to pick out a keyword in an objective and tell what they learned that relates to the word.
- If you created and saved virtual whiteboard charts, drawings, or doodles (see Strategy 9), post them as files or slides. Ask participants to find a file that relates to something they learned. Using screen share, they can pull up the chart and explain what they learned.
- Pick a participant to share one thing they learned. They then get to pick the name of the next participant who shares what they learned. Repeat until all participants have responded.
- Ask participants to create an action plan to implement the content of your session in their department (see Strategy 22).

- Conduct a review competition. Have participants design quizzes and try to stump their colleagues.
- Using a virtual whiteboard, have participants create a colorful, creative chart on an aspect of the session. They can use pictures or words. Allow the participants to explain their diagrams.
- Pick out several quotes that relate to your session. Ask the participants how the quote connects to the learning objectives or let them work in smaller groups to discuss one quote and then share their ideas with the others. Alternatively, have the participants find a quote or meme to share and explain.
- Using paper (and holding it up to video), virtual whiteboards and screen share, or file uploads, have participants draw several bubbles on a page and write one learning objective in each bubble. Instruct them to write as many things as possible that they learned about that objective surrounding the bubbles. Then have them draw lines between bubbles and indicate how the objectives relate to each other. The participants can also complete this mind mapping activity collaboratively.
- Play bingo with concepts from the learning objectives. Choose a random participant after each concept is called and ask them to give an example or describe what they learned related to that concept. You could also ask them how the idea called relates to the previous concept. There are free bingo generators online.
- Give the participants a learning objective. Have them list everything they learned about that topic or idea. Ask the participants to read their answers. They would give themselves a point if they wrote an answer no one else wrote. The person with the most points "wins" (and could potentially earn a raffle item. See Strategy 5).

A dynamic facilitator will create a purposeful and impactful ending to their course.

Conclusion

End your class strong by providing closure. Have participants review material they learned or information they found exciting. Make sure the participants have strategies to apply the course content to their specific work environment. If there are any misconceptions, address them before the participants leave. Use this time to confirm that the attendees met the learning objectives.

Apply This Strategy

- List one idea above that you can use to close your training courses.
- How well does your course demonstrate the relationship between the content or learning objectives? What could you do to help participants make meaningful connections throughout your session?

Strategy 22: Follow Up with Post-Work

Suppose a novice driver attended a four-hour PowerPoint lecture on how to drive and without practicing any driving skills received their driver's license. That would be disconcerting!

However, that is often how corporate training works. Participants attend a lecture, receive a certificate, and go back to work. They never practice or apply the skills or objectives of the training.

Now think about how novice drivers actually learn how to drive. After the classroom lessons, beginner drivers go out on the roads with their instructor and apply the concepts they just learned in class. They practice driving skills, gain mastery, and build confidence. When the instructor determines that they have mastered all of the skills needed to drive safely, they allow the student to take the driver's exam.

Drivers education classes can provide a model for learning. The objective of driving classes is to help the student learn how to operate the car safely.

Corporate training aims to help employees maximize their skills so they can contribute to the business' success. Therefore, every trainer must ask the question: What must the learner be able to apply after this course? And then: What supports will the participant need as they learn to use those skills?

Training that drives behavioral change and impacts business metrics includes a follow-up application period to cement the intended behavioral changes.[21] The application phase is often not a part of corporate training, but it can contribute to a significant portion of the learning experience.

Incorporating post-work in your training design provides an avenue for participants to apply what they learn. With your support, post-work activities help the learner practice and gain skill mastery to meet intended performance goals. While you may not have the authority if you are not their manager to ensure they complete the tasks, you can still provide the right framework for skill acquisition. You can also enroll senior leaders to coach the participants as they practice their newly-learned skills in their work setting.

Below are methods you can use in a virtual environment to support your participants as they apply the learning objectives from your course.

Make an Action Plan. At the end of the session, compile a plan with a clear outline of actions and timing.

Provide One-on-One Skills Coaching. If the group is small enough, meet with each participant individually. Coach them through how they can apply your course content directly to their unit or job position.

Provide opportunities for the participants to apply what they have learned

---

Offer Additional Resources. Provide the participant with additional resources they can use to continue the learning.

Prepare for Failure. Planning to fail sounds counterintuitive, but it is a vital aspect of the learning process. Imagine a middle-school girl in the basement practicing the violin and her mother wincing every time she hits the wrong note. Now imagine that girl on stage performing a breath-taking first-violin solo in the orchestra. There is no way to master a skill without failing while practicing. Share this analogy with your participants. Humans are hard-wired to fear failure, and your participants are no exception. If they fail while trying to implement what you have taught in your training, they will instinctively revert to prior behaviors. Coach both them AND their supervisors to expect failure as they practice to implement what you have taught them.

Find Low-Stake Practice Opportunities. Work with the participant and their supervisor to identify low-stake opportunities for them to practice the skills you have taught them.

Provide Resources for Reflection. Reflection is an essential aspect of mastering a skill, especially ones that include behavioral change. Provide ways for participants to reflect on how they are implementing the objectives. For example, if you coached middle managers on how to give a performance review, check-in with them after the annual review period. Provide them a list of questions: What went well? In what areas could you approve? What made implementing our strategy difficult? The reflection can be through a phone or video call, by email, or in a journaling aspect of your learning management system.

Connect Training to Business Metric. The goal of corporate training is to establish or improve a business metric. Why was the training conducted? In the example above, middle managers received training on conducting employee reviews as part of an initiative to decrease employee turnover. Conduct an annual assessment—if the managers are successfully implementing the strategies taught in their training, what impact is it having on turnover rates? Share that data with the middle managers and their supervisors (see Strategy 23).

Conclusion

For training to be impactful, the participants must apply what they have learned to their position. In the follow-up period, you can provide support as they practice and grow in their skills on the job. Provide times for reflection and analysis. Encourage supervisors to give feedback to the participants. Prepare the attendee for failure and celebrate their successes. Practicing is the only way to improve a skill. Design a work environment where your course participants can practice and master their skills.

Apply This Strategy

- After students leave your training course, how do you know if they are implementing the skills you have taught them?
- How can you work with the senior leaders at your organization to provide application opportunities after the training sessions have concluded?

Strategy 23: Assess the Training Effectiveness

You want to evaluate the impact of your course after its conclusion.[21] There are several reasons why evaluation is necessary. You can assess your class to improve the quality of the training.

Participant and stakeholder input can provide valuable information as to how to enhance the delivery, satisfaction, and enjoyment of the course. You can also evaluate if your participants increased their knowledge or improved upon skills in your class. Did the participants walk away having learned something new after your course? Additionally, you want to determine if the training is successful. Does the training produce the intended results? Another reason to evaluate a course is to justify the costs. Is the course valuable? Does your class provide a return-on-interest to the company's financial and the employees' time investments?

You want to use your assessments to determine:
- Were your participants engaged?
- Was there an increase in the participants' knowledge or skills after your course?
- Did the participants change their behaviors in their job settings?
- Did the participants' behavioral changes result in improved business metrics?

> **Engaged Learners → Increased Knowledge →**
> **Changed Behaviors → Improved Business Metrics**

Unfortunately, most organizations only evaluate participants' satisfaction. They less commonly assess skill acquisition, changed behaviors, or improvements to business outcomes. A dynamic facilitator knows that engaging their participants is not only for the attendees' enjoyment but rather because engagement is the lynchpin for sustained learning that positively impacts targeted business metrics.

Kirkpatrick summarizes the reasons for course assessments in his Four-Level Training Effectiveness Model.[1] He calls the assessment levels:
1. Reaction
2. Learning
3. Behavior
4. Results

The following provides suggestions on how to implement these levels of assessment in your virtual training courses.

Reaction

Reaction refers to how satisfied the participants were in the course. Did they find it enjoyable and engaging? Was it relevant to their job? Did they find the time they invested in the course valuable? Reactions can be assessed periodically throughout or at the end of the course. Evaluating reaction mid-course might allow you to adjust facilitation styles based on your participants' needs (see Strategy 28). Here are some suggestions for assessing the participants' reactions:
- Include a survey at the end of your course with Likert-type or open-ended questions
- Conduct a plus/delta discussion (or writing prompt). Ask the participants what aspects of the course contributed to their learning experience. Then ask what portions of the class they would recommend modifying or altering.
- Provide the learning objectives to the participants. Through discussion or open-ended survey questions, ask what activities they would change if they were the course facilitator.
- For a mid-course assessment, place participants into breakout groups based on learning styles. Ask them to give feedback as to whether they are enjoying and grasping the material based on their learning style or if they have suggestions for improvement.

Learning

Learning refers to increases in the participants' knowledge, skills, or abilities as a result of attending the course. When you assess learning, you can also evaluate the participants' confidence and commitment levels to implement what they have learned to their specific position[1]. A pre-test will provide you valuable information about the participants' knowledge level before your course. If most of the attendees are knowledgeable about the material you were planning to present, you can move toward more application activities or adjust your session timing to focus on the content they do not know.

- Use a quiz feature to conduct a pre-test and a post-test to assess improvements in participants' knowledge.
- Use video conferences or recordings to evaluate participants' skills at the beginning and end of your course. Using a rubric can help you objectively assess skills.
- Ask participants to rate their confidence and commitment to implement the learning objectives on a scale of 1-10. You can use a polling response system for synchronous courses or a quick quiz for asynchronous classes.

Behavior

Behavior refers to changes the participant makes in their every-day actions to apply the knowledge, skills, or abilities they just learned. For an employee to sustain behavioral changes over time, they often need to receive positive reinforcement or encouragement. The follow-up period is crucial to assisting participants in applying and mastering the behavioral changes[21] (see Strategy 22).

Behavioral assessments take place after the course has finished. Several appraisals over a period of time may be worthwhile. Implementing a post-course assessment will usually require the support of organizational leadership. The following are methods that you can use to assess behavioral changes virtually:

- Interviews via phone or videoconference.
- Self-evaluations.
- Reflection journaling.
- Supervisor evaluations. These can be submitted through email or an LMS. Initial assessments for changes in employee behavior based on the training should be used only for learning and improvement, not for performance evaluations.
- Video recording of skills or demonstrations of action changes in the participants' work environment.

Measure reaction, learning, behavior, and results

Results

The results refer to the overall reason why the company invested in the course. What underlying business metrics did the company hope to impact through the course? It often can take time for changes in employees' actions to shift business metrics. Therefore, short-term measurements can help determine if the training is having the desired impact while you monitor long-term results. Below are some suggestions when evaluating the results of the training at the organizational level.

- Connect course content to related business metrics.
- Ensure that employees have support from the organization's administration to implement course content.

- Identify smaller short-term metrics to determine if employee actions are progressing in the right direction.
- Allow enough time to pass before measuring business outcomes.
- Annual evaluations and other longitudinal data can show improvements over time.

Conclusion

You can determine the success of your course by measuring four factors: enjoyment, knowledge or skill improvements, behavioral change, and business outcomes. You can ask the participants how satisfied they are with your course. You can use pre- and post-tests to measure changes in skills or knowledge. In the follow-up period, you can assess how many participants have changed their daily actions as a result of your course. Lastly, you can monitor related business metrics. You want to evaluate all four factors to show the value and effectiveness of your course.

Apply This Strategy

- Choose one evaluation from the "Learning" level to embed into your course.
- Talk with senior leaders and determine if there is one or two short-term and long-term business metrics that relate to your course that you can monitor.

Strategy 24: Structure Your Course: Putting It All Together

It is strategic to structure your course in an outline form before implementation. You will be able to visualize the overarching scope of your course when you plan it out. Once you type your outline, you can move the ideas around or substitute activities if you do not like the sequencing. It is much easier to modify the outline than to move content around in your LMS.

It may be tempting to start with writing or recording the course content. However, you have several planning tasks before that step.

You will want to start with the WHY and, subsequently, the course objectives. Then identify the targeted participants of your course. How many participants are likely to be in each class? What are their levels of expertise? Decide how and when you will evaluate the learning objectives as that can guide your session structure and choice of activities.

The training course should be strategically designed to guide the participants to master the course objectives

---

You then strategically plan the content of your course with the intent to guide your participants to master the learning objectives. Outline your sessions and plan activities in roughly twenty-minute increments (see Strategy 19). Add another level of sub-bullets with the why, what, and how for each activity. You can add notes about the technology you will use and the resources you need. Describe what pre-work and post-work is appropriate for the context of your course. Now you are ready to begin creating your lectures, recordings, and activities.

Below is a sample flowchart for a virtual course planning process.

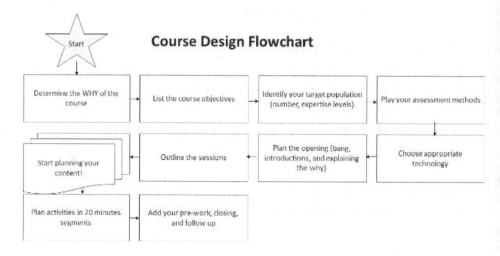

The following is a sample outline for a training course showing supervisors how to use a new performance review system. Notice how the sections are planned in twenty-minute segments.

Example Outline
Online Training for Supervisors to Learn Updated Employee Performance Review System
Total Time: 2 hours

WHY of the Course: Employee satisfaction surveys indicated that employees felt their performance reviews were not relevant to their positions. They noted that the supervisors rushed through or did not explain their performance rating. Several supervisors had made errors when inputting data in the performance portal, causing confusion and delays in raises and promotions. The Human Resource Department invested in an updated Review Assessment questions and rubrics. The end goal of this training is for better implementation of the annual performance reviews. A secondary goal is for employees to understand their performance ratings better and increase or maintain high levels of performance.

Course Learning Objectives:
By the end of this training course, the supervisors will be able to:
1) Describe the contents of the performance review and use a rubric to assess employee performance
2) Coach an employee through the performance review in a constructive manner
3) Enter performance review data in the human resource portal

Open with a Bang and Why, What, and How of the Course (20 minutes)
- Open with a Bang: Show a movie clip of a poorly conducted employee evaluation. Tell participants that is what you hope to help them avoid and the course will teach them how to conduct reviews in a constructive manner.
- Icebreaker: Play "employee evaluation bingo" on video conference
- Show the why: Provide data as to how employee evaluations relate to turnover rates and productivity
- Outline the agenda, explain the learning objectives, and describe the active learning strategies

Introduction (20 minutes)
- Show introductory video
- Ask participants to review the new evaluation questions and rubric and compare the new evaluation form to the old assessment. Ask which questions were added or removed and which line items might be confusing.

Demonstration (20 minutes)
- Demonstrate how to mark the answers in the online portal. Provide information regarding three imaginary employees (outstanding employee, poor employee, average employee) to the participants. As you demonstrate how to use the portal, have the participants guide you on filling out the rubric.

- Divide participants into groups and give them a case study. Give them portal login and access, and have them complete the employee assessment online for their test employee.

Discussion (20 minutes)

- On a shared document, have participants list problems they have faced when conducting employee evaluations
- Share different approaches for in-person evaluation discussions. As you explain each tactic, use a highlighter on the shared document to indicate which fear or problem the method solved.

Application (20 minutes)

- Complete a role-play activity. Have two participants act as the supervisor and the employee. Provide them with a scenario and have the supervisor review the evaluation with the employee. The rest of the participants watch via video conference. Ask the remaining participants to discuss what the supervisor did well and what they could improve. Complete two or three scenarios.

Closing/Debrief (20 minutes)

- Facilitate a group discussion. Ask them to explain the key takeaways from the training. Use a virtual whiteboard to list their answers.
- Have participants fill out a planning document. Provide them with the significant dates and steps for the new review system. Ask them to fill in dates for when they plan to complete tasks.

Post-Work

- Provide participants with a reflection worksheet specific to the material you presented. Ask the participants to fill out the reflection after each employee review they conduct.
- Schedule a call with the participants after the employee reviews are due. Ask the participant what went well and was awkward during the evaluations. Have the participant list two things they are going to work on to improve during the next round of reviews.

Conclusion

Do not rush to the course content. Set up the framework for your course first. Start with the purpose of the course and the learning objectives. Identify factors such as the number of participants. Decide what types of activities you want to implement and which technology is the most suitable. Then move into course content. Organize first before creating.

Apply This Strategy

- Do not begin writing (or editing) course content until you identify the why of the course and the learning objectives.
- Type a basic outline for your class. Then, add more details regarding activity instructions (why, what, and how), the technology you will use, and the resources you need.

Part 4: Implementing Personal Facilitation Effectiveness

Strategy 25: Present with Ease

Newscasters confidently look at a camera with great posture and body awareness as they talk.
TED Talk presenters effortlessly command the stage as they present.
Social media influencers gracefully pop on their live streams to update their followers.

A common factor between the newscasters, TED Talk presenters, and social media influencers is that they make presenting look easy. In reality, they all have spent time practicing to be on camera. Newscasters spend years learning how to move, speak, use their hands, and adjust their voice. TED Talk presenter practice their presentations over and over. Social medial influencers review videos, change angles, and learn techniques to look good on camera.

When you present in your course, you want to project as much confidence as possible with your body language and voice. Below are several ideas to help you look professional and put you and your participants at ease. Record your sessions and take note of how well you do in the following areas.

Hands
- If you are charting, hold the stylus.
- Keep your hand primarily on the top of the desk when recording or live. Avoid putting your elbow on the table and touching your jaw.
- Rest your elbows on your hips and touch your fingers together if you stand while presenting or recording
- Use your hands expressively at the appropriate times, but not so much that it distracts the participants.
- Avoid adjusting clothing, touching your face or hair, or tapping a table.

Eyes and Face
- Know where the camera is on your device(s). Look directly at the camera, not at your screen.
- Smile. Look like you are enjoying yourself.
- Relax your jaw.
- Do not be afraid to use expressive faces.

Posture
- Sit up tall or stand up straight.
- Do not slouch.
- Drop the shoulders.

Moving
- If you are sitting while recording or going live, ensure you are not jiggling a leg, turning side-to-side or swaying, or making any other repetitive motion.
- If you are standing, face the camera unless writing on a whiteboard. Avoid leaning against the wall or making repetitive motions. Move around slightly, but be aware of how far you can move while being in view.
- If you have any props, objects, or papers, make sure they are within hands reach so that whether you are sitting or standing you do not need to leave the view of the camera while recording or presenting live.
- Remove barriers between you and the camera. If you need a place for notes, put them on a table or off to your side.

Dynamic facilitators spend time practicing to present with ease

Voice
- Vary the pace and intensity of your voice.
- Slightly speed up or slow down the cadence of your speech to emphasize points.
- Talk neither too loud nor too soft.
- Avoid filler words (see Strategy 26).

Although it can be awkward, watch your recordings or presentations. Go through the list above and reflect on what you do well when presenting and what you can correct. You will start to see steady improvements as you are conscious of how you look and act.

Conclusion

They make it look easy, but the best presenters have spent time practicing their delivery. Be cognizant of your body, movements, and posture while talking. Smile at the camera. Vary the tone and cadence of your speech. While it may be awkward to watch recordings of yourself, it is the best way to identify the areas for improvement.

Apply This Strategy
- Practice recording yourself standing or sitting (how you will be presenting) for five minutes. Review the recording. Pick one to two areas to focus on and be mindful of when teaching.
- After each course, review some of your recorded material. Use the Personal Facilitation Checklist (see Appendix C) to evaluate yourself.

Strategy 26: Speak with Confidence by Reducing Filler Words

Speakers convey confidence and authority when they speak without filler words. However, not using filler words is a challenge for most speakers and facilitators. Some of the most common filler words are:

- Um
- Ah
- Sort of
- Ya Know
- Some
- Really

- Kind of
- Like
- So
- Little
- Right
- Ok

Filler words have minimal value and diminish your message. Dynamic facilitators work to minimize the filler words they use.

Below are some techniques you can use to identify and reduce your filler words.

- Record yourself presenting and listen for filler words. Figure out which expressions you are more prone to use.
- Ask a colleague to review one of your recordings and list your filler words.
- Pick one filler word you use often. Consciously attempt to reduce how many times you use it. If you had 15 "ums" in your first session, set a goal for 10 "ums" in the next class.
- Practice presenting your session and specifically focus on eliminating the filler words. Choose appropriate alternative words and practice inserting them into the correct locations during your presentation.
- After a sentence, *consciously close your lips* for one second. Take the time to reset and to think about the beginning word of your next sentence. A short, silent pause between sentences is a

powerful way to reduce superfluous words and increase the effectiveness of your statement.

Examples:

Change From These Sentences:	To These Sentences:
"So, like, one thing that we *kind of* do when driving is get distracted by, *you know,* signs."	"When driving, we often get distracted by signs."
"So, um, now we will watch a little video."	"Watch the video and identify three ways the leader gives feedback."

Speakers portray confidence and authority when they speak without filler words

---

Conclusion

You sound confident and authoritative when you do not use filler words. However, many presenters have one or more words they often use while talking. Identify which filler words you tend to use. Actively work on reducing the use of those words each time you present.

Apply This Strategy

- Identify your most commonly used filler words.
- Create a tally sheet for a filler word you use often. Each time you conduct a session, aim for a new low score record of saying the word.

Strategy 27: Avoid the Dreaded Silence

At some point, all facilitators have faced total silence and blank-faced stares from participants. The quietness can be awkward, and facilitators often jump back in to avoid the silence. Online sessions where participants silently hide behind their screens can present a particular challenge for getting them to speak up.

A dynamic facilitator knows how to mitigate the silence. From designing strategic icebreakers to energizing the session with active learning exercises, great facilitators set up their courses to be conducive to great discussions.

Here are some techniques to manage the dreaded silence in a synchronous virtual setting.

Be Comfortable in the Silence
After asking a question, learn to be comfortable with up to eight seconds of silence. It seems like a lifetime, but participants may need this wait time to process their thoughts.

Tell Them to Write the Answer First
Ask a question and have the participants respond to a poll or write their answer down at home or on a shared document. Responding first gives them time to think. Then ask them to reply to the question verbally. You will almost always get a response. You can also call on a person and say, "Juan, what did you write down?"

Assign Partner Discussions
Use a partner discussion for the participants to answer a question. Assign groups to chat for five minutes in a breakout room on video conferencing. Then bring everyone back together and ask groups to share. This approach is helpful for answers that can have multiple perspectives or are

complicated. Group responses reduce pressure as the answer comes from the group as opposed to the individual.

Ask Clear Questions

Ensure the question is clearly worded. If needed, write the question on a virtual whiteboard or slide. If there seems to be confusion, restate the questions.

Dynamic facilitators have strategies to mitigate the silence

Affirm the Answers

If you thank the participant for their input, they will continue to engage. If you have no response or one that indicates the person was wrong, they may hesitate in subsequent discussions.

>   Examples of positive affirmations:
>> *Thank you, Anne. Your answer is insightful in helping us see a more in-depth view of this issue.*
>> *That is perfect, Dan. Dan highlighted a point that I did not think about but is very powerful.*

>   Examples of responses that may shut down future participation:
>> *Ok. Does anyone else have an answer?*
>> *I am not sure that is right. Who else can try?*

Ask Open-Ended Questions

Participants can answer a closed question with a yes/no response. An open-ended question is one where the participant has to think about their answer and respond with more than a single word.

Asking: *"Have you ever had a bad experience on an airplane?"* will only get head nods.

Change this question to an open-ended question such as: *"What was your worst experience while flying?"* and you will get better answers.

Follow up with Probing Questions
You can use probing questions to prod participants to think more deeply about their answers. Probing questions can also be used if the initial response was vague or ambiguous. The following are examples of probing questions.

> *Why do you think that will work?*
> *What kind of impact do you think that solution would have?*
> *How did you come to that conclusion?*

Break Up Long Lectures
If you talk for a long time, participants will shift to a passive mode. If you ask a question near the end of your lecture, disengaged participants who may not have been following the conversation will not be able to contribute right away.

Ensure you insert an active segment into a more extended section of talking. Ask a question, have the participants write something in a workbook or type into a fillable PDF, or have them pair up for a minute to reflect on the content.

Ask Them to Review Their Notes
Rather than ask, *"Does anyone have a question"*?

Try:

"We just processed a large amount of material in the last twenty minutes. Look at your notes and write down one thought that comes to mind." You can then ask for a couple of comments, which will have a higher probability of a response.

Tell Them to Summarize

A masterful technique that will keep everyone's attention even while lecturing is to put them on their toes. Tell the group you will go over several concepts in the session. Every few minutes, you will pause and pick a name out of a hat. The participant whose name you call will have to summarize the main idea of what you just went over. You will find people taking notes, asking questions, and being laser-focused. Do not overuse this method, but applying this technique several times in a day works well.

Conclusion

The online environment can create an intimidating setting if participants do not respond to questions. Don't be afraid of the silence. It may take a few seconds for participants to answer. Also, there are several techniques you can use to avoid silence. Giving the participants time to write down their responses first, asking open-ended and probing questions, and having them summarize their notes can initiate conversations. If someone does contribute, affirm their input.

Apply This Strategy

- The next time you ask a question and no one response right away, count to ten slowly under your breath. Chances are someone will answer before you get to ten.
- Pick one technique from the list above to implement in your next training course.

Strategy 28: Adapt to Varied Learning Preferences

Each participant comes to your training with their unique learning style. Everyone has different ways in which they process information. Attendees also learn at different speeds. Some will grasp the material quickly, while others will need more time to master the content. Their experience levels also will likely vary. Experienced attendees will be able to more quickly grasp the learning objectives than those with less experience. Some participants may enjoy active learning, and others may initially feel awkward with the interaction.

The dynamics of each different training session will vary based on the unique combination of participants and their learning preferences.

Because the participants in each of your courses learn differently, and your goal is to help those students master the knowledge or skills you are presenting, in theory, you should tailor *every session* to meet your participants' needs. Dynamic facilitators are experts at adapting the presentation of their material or activities as they are running courses based on their attendees' learning styles.

To be clear: This is an advanced facilitating skill. Leading a session well when you have a set agenda and a clear plan for activities can be a challenge in and of itself. Modifying sessions during the course to meet the participants' unique needs requires sophisticated improvising. If you are not at this skill level, do not be intimidated. It takes a master facilitator to adjust a session seamlessly while the course is in process.

Below are some ideas to help you identify your participants' learning needs and suggestions on adjusting course delivery. As you facilitate your courses, try one or two of these suggestions. Reflect on what worked well for you. As you practice consciously considering your participants' learning needs and implementing some of the techniques listed here, you will improve your ability to make your classes the ideal learning environment for any learner.

- Post a survey as part of the course pre-work. Use that survey to gather information on the participants' baseline knowledge of the course material and experience level. Use that data to plan your activities.
- Conduct an icebreaker or poll at the beginning of your course that focuses on learning styles. That information can help you identify the type of learning activities those participants will most prefer.
- When you present your agenda, explain that you will be using active learning exercises throughout the course. Sometimes a short demonstration can illustrate that active learning is more effective for information recall than passive learning. If your attendees seem resistant to active learning techniques, this may help them "buy-in" to this learning approach.

Adapt your content to the specific learning needs of your participants

---

- Not everyone in the course may have experience or be comfortable using different modes of technology. If you plan an exercise using software that several participants are unfamiliar with, choose an alternate activity for that learning objective. If they have to spend an excessive amount of time navigating the software, they may spend more time learning the technology than the intended skill.
- When planning your sessions, list and prepare one to two alternative activities for each learning objective. As you get a feel

for the dynamics of your group, you can substitute activities if needed.

- Some attendees like experiential learning, while others prefer direct instruction and hands-on practice. Determine which type of exercise best suits the intended learning outcome. Provide a rationale for exercise. A logical explanation can help a resistant participant engage in learning styles they do not enjoy.
- There may be participants who come to your course with more experience than other attendees. Some attendees may learn the material quicker than others. Recruit these participants to help teach part of the session or allow them to share their advice.
- If a participant seems disconnected, they may be disengaged or might process information slowly. Find a way to connect with them to determine the appropriate facilitation adjustment.
- If your course requires that the participants master a specific physical skill, some participants may learn it quickly, while others may need more repetition. Plan flexible scheduling. Move on quicker if everyone learns the skills fast; add extra time if several participants need additional practice.
- Use polling or quiz applications in small spurts throughout your session to determine if the participants are grasping the material. If a majority of the class is getting answers correct, move quickly through the material. If the participants' responses vary, take it as a sign that multiple attendees are not understanding the content and spend more time (add one of your back-up activities) in that session.

Conclusion

Learning is difficult, and everyone learns differently. As the "guide on the side," your goal is to identify and implement the most effective learning strategies for the unique group of learners each time you lead a session. It may even require adapting learning strategies for different participants within the same session. Use a pre-course quiz to identify learning styles. Use a flexible schedule and plan alternative activities to give you the ability to adjust the course as needed.

Apply This Strategy

- Based on your course content and delivery method, what is one thing you can add to the beginning of your class to identify the learning needs or experience levels of your participants?
- As you facilitate the next course, attempt one small modification to your class based on the learning needs of your participants.

Part 5: Minimizing Facilitation Inhibitors

Strategy 29: Break the Facilitation Fear

Many people have a fear of facilitating training. Whether you conduct a one-hour webinar or a multi-day program, preparing and implementing a training course can be stressful and intimidating. You want the participants to enjoy the course. You want it to be worth the time they are investing. And above all, you want the training to be useful.

But being a facilitator means speaking in front of others. It requires giving clear instructions and coordinating activities. You must encourage, cajole, adapt, teach, and respond effortlessly. In the virtual environment, you are also competing for the participants' attention despite digital distractions, engaging attendees through a screen, and navigating technology. You need to manage technology and applications.

Simultaneously managing these details can be overwhelming and leave the facilitator more focused on themselves than on the needs of the learner. However, to ensure that all participants master the learning objectives, the facilitator has to be able to focus more on the learners than on themselves.

The following graphic demonstrates four stages of facilitating:

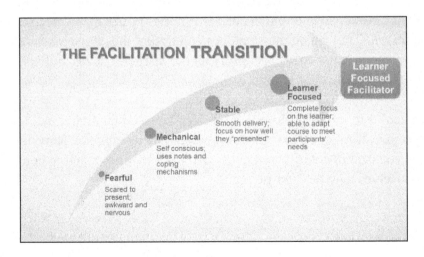

Stage 1: A Fearful Facilitator is scared to death to present in front of others. They feel awkward and nervous. They are scared of the technology and virtual environment. Their focus is entirely on themselves and not the learners. As a result, the training is stilted and uncomfortable for all involved.

Stage 2: A Mechanical Facilitator has to figure out coping mechanisms to get through the training course. They often have scripted lines and need to follow a rigorous agenda. They move the participants through the course with less awkwardness than fearful facilitators, but they are very conscious of themselves and the minutia details during the entire training.

Stage 3: A Stable Facilitator smoothly delivers the training material. They can make jokes and small adaptations to the content. The participants are engaged and enjoy learning. However, this facilitator still has a significant focus on themselves as the "entertainer. They evaluate themselves on how well they "presented."

Stage 4: A Learner-Focused Facilitator concentrates wholly on the participants' needs. They identify the unique learning preferences of the attendees and can modify course activities. They are aware of who is bored, who has mastered the content, and who is struggling to learn. This facilitator effectively communicates WHY these participants need to learn the material. They guide the attendees and ensure they have mastered all of the content. Their focus is entirely on the learners' needs and not on themselves during the training.

Your goal is to move as close to a Learner-Focused facilitator as possible. Speaking in front of others, appearing unknowledgeable, or worrying things you cannot control are factors that keep facilitators more conscious of themselves than their participants.

Below are some general presentation strategies to cope with the usual fears that accompany facilitating. Using these tips will help you become more comfortable in your role as a facilitator, enabling you to focus more on your learners than on yourself.

Remember, It Is Not About You
Refer back to Strategy 2. It is not about how well you performed but rather how well the participants mastered the course content.

Throw the Monkey
At the beginning of a session, many facilitators experience the "fight or flight" physiological response of a pounding heart, dry throat, and shaking hands. John Townsend[22] describes this feeling as "if a monkey has suddenly jumped onto your shoulders. He claws at your neck and weighs you down, making your knees feel weak." Townsend's solution is to "Throw the Monkey," which means to transfer the problem to someone else. In regard to presenting, "throw the monkey" refers to asking the audience to do an activity. Within the first thirty seconds of your presentation, conduct a poll, have everyone do the same action on screen, or ask a volunteer to participate in a quick activity. Temporarily transferring the focus to the audience allows you time to relax, take a deep breath, and prepare to address the group.

You Do Not Need to Know Everything
No matter how great a facilitator you are or how much you have prepared, it is likely that one day you will receive a question that you cannot answer. If you have a fear of appearing not to know everything, give yourself grace. One, it is impossible to know everything. Do your research and know your material, but give yourself permission to not know everything. Two, it is fine to say things like:

- "That's a good question. Let me look it up, and I will get back to you."

- "Wow, I've never thought of that angle. What a good perspective. Let me think about that."
- "Great question. What do you think could be the solution?"

Use Humor

Humor can be a great way to smooth missteps. A short quip after you make a mistake can diffuse the awkwardness. Remind yourself that it is acceptable to make a mistake (all facilitators do at some point). Laugh it off, and your participants will laugh with you. Here are some examples:

Called out for misspelling a word on a virtual whiteboard or PowerPoint?	Say, "I was seeing if you were paying attention!"
Fielded several tough questions in a row that you do not know?	Say, "Looks like I'm leaving here with homework tonight!"
Lost your train of thought or paused too long?	Say, "Just taking a mental pause!"
Accidently gave incorrect instructions?	Say, "I was just checking to see if you could follow instructions! You passed that test. Now, here is what you actually need to do."
Your audio cut out?	When it is back on, say, "We thought we would try lip reading this session!"

Master facilitators are more focused on the learners than on themselves

Keep an Outline Nearby

The best facilitators are not reading off the script. They know what the learning objectives are and what passive and active exercises they are conducting each session. They are aware of the ideal pace for the course. An outline can help you stay on track. If you are closer to a mechanical or stable facilitator, you may need more details on your framework. You can include opening sentences, activity instructions, or transition phrases on your outline. As you move closer to a learner-focused facilitator, you may realize you only need keywords. If your mind goes blank or you think the session is starting to derail, quickly glance at your outline and re-focus.

Smile

If you are very focused on the task at hand—facilitating—it can be easy to use a default concentrated facial expression. Work on consciously smiling and relaxing your shoulders during the session. When you smile, your body will release endorphins and reduce stress. Taking a deep breath, dropping your shoulders, and unclenching your jaw releases tension as well. These small actions trick your brain into relaxing. The more you can relax and enjoy yourself, the more you will be able to focus on your learners instead of being very self-aware.

- Smile when the first attendee logs on and when you greet a new participant.
- When the participants are doing an active learning exercise (and you are not the center of the stage), take a deep breath, and relax your shoulders.
- Every time you look at the clock to check the time, smile.
- Reset right before you start a session or bring a group back from an activity. Smile, drop your shoulders, and unclench your jaw.

Conclusion

Great presenters are more focused on their learners than on themselves. They use strategies such as humor to defuse awkward situations. They "throw the monkey" to relieve anxiety at the beginning of the course. Their bodies are relaxed, and they admit when they do not have all of the answers. While they present smoothly, these facilitators concentrate entirely on helping the participants meet the learning objectives.

Apply This Strategy

- Which type of facilitator do you best identify with? What is one thing you could practice to help you move toward being a learner-focused trainer?
    - __Total Fear
    - __Mechanical
    - __Stable
    - __Learner Focused
- Choose a quick "Throw the Monkey" activity to use during your next session.
- If you depend on notes or a script, choose one session during your next course to ad-lib.
- Outline your presentation with key points. Practice. Record the actual session and review. Ask yourself what you could do to improve.
- Watch a recording of one of your courses. Does it look like you are having fun? Evaluate your body language, posture, and smile. Identify any changes you need to make.

Strategy 30: Minimize Participant Resistance

Facilitators often face resistance from course participants. This resistance can take the form of argumentative challenges, reluctance to complete activities, or body language indicating annoyance. Other participants may sit silently "putting in the time' while checked out mentally. Unrestricted, the resistance can cause a course to be uncomfortable and prevent the attendees from fully mastering the course objectives.

There are several reasons why a participant may be resistant to the training:
- They think they do not have anything new to learn
- They feel they are more knowledgeable than you
- They consider the training session a waste of time
- They fear learning a new skill
- They believe the material is irrelevant to their position

As a facilitator, your role is to engage the participants and identify the underlying reason for their resistance. Then, you have to find the right approach to demonstrate the value of the training as it relates to their opposition. For example, if the participant thinks the course is irrelevant to their position, you have to make it clear that the content will impact their day-to-day responsibilities.

Below are stories of participants displaying each of the types of resistance. The stories include examples of how the facilitator uncovered the reason for their opposition, countered the challenge, and engaged the participant in the course.

I Don't Have Anything to Learn Here

On the first morning of a three-day leadership training course, Marques logged in a few minutes early. He had a scowl on his face and his arms folded across his face.

The facilitator introduced himself and welcomed him to the course. Marques told the facilitator, "No offense, but I have been a supervisor for twenty years. There is nothing you can teach me in three days that I do not already know."

The facilitator nodded. "I count on experienced leaders sharing ideas and real-world experiences during the sessions to help the newer leaders. Could you see yourself as a coach for the next three days? Instead of seeing yourself as a learner, please share ideas where appropriate." Marques grunted. The facilitator smiled and then greeted the next attendee who had logged in.

When the class started, Marques had relaxed his arms but still was scowling. During the first day, a participant asked for advice for a challenging situation. The facilitator looked at Marques and said, "Marques, you have been here for a long time. Have you faced that issue here? Could you provide any advice?"
Over the next three days, Marques' demeanor slowly started changing. He became engaged and enthusiastic. He added insightful stories and advice throughout the sessions.

When the course ended, everyone provided a closing comment. Marques said, "I did not want to attend this course, but this was the greatest experience of my career. I did not realize I could learn so much. I only have two years until I retire. I was coasting to the finish. Now, I see what an impact I could have in the next two years. I can coach and mentor new leaders to grow and take this site to the next level."

Facilitation Strategies
- Listen to understand their resistance.
- Validate their experience.
- Ask them to share their insight.
- Place them as virtual breakout group leaders or discussion monitors.

- Get them to provide examples, suggestions, and advice.
- Ask them to be a mentor for those with less experience.

I Know More Than You

A facilitator was responsible for training operators on several operating programs for their unit. The facilitator had designed online modules and exams that the operators had to complete as part of their qualification.

One day, the facilitator was working when she received a phone call from Big Jim, a senior-level operator. "I HAVE GOT A PROBLEM," Big Jim shouted. "Your training and tests are terrible. I took a test, and I got all the right answers, but the program said I failed. Now I have to do the entire test over again. I QUIT!"

The facilitator knew Big Jim had a gruff exterior but that he was also a smart and quick learner.
The facilitator asked Big Jim to schedule a time to look over the quiz questions. Using a screen share, they logged into the test together. Big Jim pointed out several items that were confusing or contained incorrect information. The facilitator asked Big Jim to go through the rest of the exams to critique the questions and the training materials.

A few weeks later, the facilitator hosted a live review and reflection session for all of the operators who had completed the modules. Two younger operators told her that Big Jim made them repeat their quizzes until they got 100% before he scheduled them as a shift leader. Another operator said that Big Jim had taken the time to work with him to master the content.

Big Jim was an influential operator. By getting his buy-in, he became an advocate for the program and accelerated the pace of the training in his unit.

Facilitating Strategies
- Listen to understand their resistance
- Do not get defensive
- Turn the situation around by getting their input
- Allow them to critique the material and assessments
- Ask them if there are knowledge or skill gaps in the material
- Get them to be an advocate instead of an adversary
- Encourage them to train others
- Be open to some of their ideas

This Training is a Waste of My Time

Athena was a mid-level leader who was assigned to take a course on developing an organizational vision. She was the first to log into a pre-session call where the facilitator introduced herself, provided the course outline, and answered questions. Athena asked, "How long will this call be? I have a fundraiser I am hosting tonight. Also, I see the session next week is from 8-3 pm. Will it last that long? I am swamped, and this course is a waste of my time."

The facilitator acknowledged her. "It sounds like you have a lot on your plate. I'd love to hear how your fundraiser goes. Can you let me know next week? Also, we sent some emails with documents and questions. If you can look that over and come to the course with some ideas, we will have a more productive session."

When Athena logged into the training session the following week, she had already pulled up the course documents. "How did your fundraiser go?" asked the facilitator?

"Great!" answered Athena. "We almost doubled the amount we raised last year. Also, as I started looking over the course material, I can see how developing a strong vision could positively impact our fundraising efforts. Many of our donors wanted to know what our future plans are and how we are going to differentiate ourselves as a company."

"That's excellent," smiled the facilitator. "I think you are going to find this afternoon's topic on communicating your vision through storytelling of particular interest.

For the entire day, Athena was enthusiastic. She took notes and added substance to the dialogue. The facilitator could tell she was excited. "I can't wait to take this back to our leadership team," Athena said. "I have so many ideas! Once we have a compelling organizational vision, we will be able to leverage it for our fundraising goals."

Facilitation Strategies
- Listen to identify the underlying cause of the resistance.
- Ensure the session does not have busywork. Make sure all meetings and activities connect to the WHY. Use the why, what, and how method to demonstrate the value of the session to the participants.
- Use pre-work for participants to review information, complete tasks, or come with ideas to make the best use of the training time.

- Pre-work surveys or conversations are useful methods to identify the participants' "pain points." Show how your training helps solve those problems.
- Connect the content to the participants' day-to-day tasks.

I am Scared

Sofia's supervisor directed her to attend an online "train-the-trainer" workshop so that she could facilitate training at their site. When she learned that she had to lead a 60-minute virtual training session during the seminar, Sofia told her boss that she was not going to attend. Her boss told her the training was part of her job responsibility. Sofia was so distraught that she told him she would resign before taking the course.
The supervisor and the course facilitator talked about the situation. The facilitator said if she would be willing to attend and participate in the workshop but still felt by the end that she could not lead the session, that he would substitute an alternative culminating exercise for her.

When Sofia logged into the live training, she was still agitated. She told the facilitator, "There is no way I can do an hour-long live session." The facilitator listened and saw the non-verbal communication of fear. He told her he completely understood her anxiety. The facilitator reassured her that she would not be required to lead the session if she did not feel ready and said there were other activities she could do instead. He also told her that the skills she would learn would help her even if she designed recorded segments for the training at her site.

Sofia relaxed slightly. The facilitator had a welcoming environment for the class. He had the participants conduct an icebreaker, reducing the tension for active learning strategies. The facilitator encouraged input and did not demeanor participants who made mistakes. Sofia found that she enjoyed the activities and discussions.

When she realized that a great facilitator conducts interactive training with active and passive learning techniques and did not need to speak for an hour straight, she worked up the nerve to attempt her mock training session.

Not only did Sofia do a phenomenal job with her mock presentation during the workshop, but she transformed her entire teaching approach. She ended up doing facilitation work more broadly for her career.

Facilitation Strategies
- Listen to understand their resistance
- Build a relationship with the participant
- Offer a variety of assessment opportunities (if applicable)

- Help the participants become comfortable with each other
- Allow them to make mistakes to grow and learn

Listen to understand the underlying reason for the resistance

---

I'll Never Use This Information

Aadir enrolled in a self-paced asynchronous supervisor development course. The facilitator noticed that Aadir seemed only to want the certificate at the end so that he would be eligible for an internal promotion. The facilitator had added active learning exercises, and it appeared that Aadir put in minimal effort.

On the evaluation at the end of the course, Aadir wrote: "This whole course was a waste of time! Nothing in this module applies to first-line supervisors. All the examples in the modules do no relate to our industry.

Also, I do not think my direct report would even allow me to do half of the leadership strategies you presented."

The facilitator followed up with Aadir with a phone call and some probing questions. "The content is good," Aadir said, "for a senior leader. But there is no way for me to implement these leadership skills."

The facilitator told Aadir that she was going to look into restructuring the course and would be in touch. The facilitator had a meeting with the company's senior leaders. She outlined the course content and asked them how they wanted front-line leaders to implement the leadership strategies. She had a senior leader make a short video on why they wanted front-line leaders to develop these skills. The Human Resource department added skills that she taught into the annual performance reviews.
The facilitator called Aadir and asked him and his colleagues to meet via video conferencing. They provided her with more specific examples to use in her content.

The following year, the facilitator offered the same course and asked Aadir to be a co-facilitator. In the beginning, they played the senior leader's video and reviewed the performance reports. The modules contained the updated examples. The participants were much more engaged. "This course was very useful for my job position!" was the feedback that year.

Facilitation Strategies
- Listen to understand the underlying cause of the resistance.
- Ensure that senior leaders will allow the trainees to use the content of your course.
- Send an email before the course with examples highlighting the value of the content for the specific group of attendees.
- Highlight the WHY very early in the course.

- Have senior leaders send emails or record videos with examples of how the organization values the course. The company must follow through with actions as well (e.g., participants using their new skills is noted positively on annual evaluations) for the participants to trust the senior leaders.
- Provide industry and position-specific examples. If you don't know enough about the industry, ask someone for input. It also means you may need to tailor your course depending on the participants.

Conclusion

You may have a participant one day who is resistant, disruptive, or challenges your expertise or content. Listen to determine the source of the resistance. Come along side of them and explain how the course content will help them even if they are scared or do not think the content will apply to them.

Apply This Strategy

- Think about a resistive participant you had previously. What do you think was the underlying cause of their resistance? What is one strategy you could have tried to reduce their resistance?
- Choose one suggestion from the case studies above that you could implement at the beginning of the course to mitigate participant resistance.

Strategy 31: Earn Their Trust

There was a four-hour live video conference session for operators at a large plant. The session topic was "Becoming a World-Class Operation." The facilitators were enthusiastic but provided no agenda or context for the course. From the very beginning, the participants started challenging the facilitator. It took an hour for the complaining to stop. Once the facilitators got the operators on track, none of them engaged in the material or exercises. When the facilitators would ask for suggestions to improve their sites, all they received were blank stares and silence.

After the course ended, the facilitators deliberated the cause of the uncooperative class. They followed up with several participants and learned that:

- The facilitators had shown pictures of world-class manufacturing sites, while the operators' plant was in disrepair.
- The operators did not believe that the leaders planned to invest in any real changes.
- Some operators had brought up safety and production concerns in the past, but their supervisors brushed them off.
- The operators saw no way to apply the content. They did not feel that they had the authority to make changes taught in the class.

In essence, the operators did not trust that the course content was of value to the company. They did not believe the senior leaders would implement the processes. They did not think supervisors would support the necessary changes.

A dynamic facilitator works to earn the participants' trust. Building trust can seem irrelevant. However, it is significant to obtain the participant's buy-in and ensure there is a behavior change after your session.

Some participants start a course with either complete distrust and resistance, demonstrated in the previous chapter (see Strategy 30). Others may be more neutral in their mindset. Very few participants log in convinced of the value of your course content and plan to invest time to implement the skills into their daily behaviors.

Distrust	Neutral	Full Trust
Resistant to ideas Unwilling to learn or try	Will leave with no takeaways No intent to implement ideas	Believes material is of value Fully intends to implement

Your goal as a facilitator is to meet each participant where they are. Distrustful and neutral participants will walk away with no intent to implement what they have learned. You want to help these participants move towards full trust because after finishing your course, your goal is for each participant to use what you taught.

Training without behavioral change is meaningless. Getting the participants to trust that the material is worth implementing is crucial.

The following are strategies you can use to help move participants from "distrust" or "neutral" to "full trust" in the process.
- Ensure the senior leadership support implementation of the course content.
- Be transparent regarding discrepancies between training material and the organization's current reality.
- Build relationships before the session begins.
- Show value for the participants.
- Connect the training to the organization's vision.

- Indicate how the organization will reward participants who follow through on implementing what they learned.

Training without behavioral change is meaningless.
Getting participants to trust that the material
is worth implementing is crucial.

How the Facilitators Built Trust

The facilitators redesigned the "Becoming a World-Class Operation" course for the next session. Before the class, they met with the senior leaders to ensure their support for the organizational transition. The leaders posted an honest email to the operators indicating that the site did not meet the criteria shown in training and admitted it would take time to evolve into a world-class operation. They stated they were willing to invest in the necessary changes.

The facilitators shared practical goals and objectives with the participants ahead of time. They called the participants to see what concerns they had before the training started so the facilitators could sense any issues or questions they could address immediately.

When the training started, the facilitators used breakout rooms on their video conference. They asked the groups to identify frustrations or waste in their area. The group wrote their answers on a virtual whiteboard and shared their screen during their time to present. The facilitators made a connection between their issues and how the training would be the foundation to reduce their concerns.

The organization began a recognition system for units that decreased waste and increased productivity. Employees who implemented ideas from the course were given "World Class" badges and received high marks on their annual performance review. Several received raises.

Conclusion

Participants must trust that applying the course material is worth their time. Earning trust starts well before the class begins by verifying that the organization supports the initiative and initiating thoughtful pre-course communication. Trust is fostered during the session as participants recognize how the content applies to their specific role. When the administration recognizes participants for making the appropriate behavioral changes in their setting, the participants solidify their trust in the process.

Apply This Strategy

- Describe the senior leader's support for the last course you implemented. Is there a disconnect between the training content and the organizational environment?
- The next time you conduct a training session, quickly identify which participants are in a state of distrust, neutral, or full trust. Apply a few strategies from this chapter to help move all the participants towards complete confidence in the training process

Conclusion

Dynamic facilitators design and orchestrate their courses to maximize the participants' learning experience. Effective training culminates in the participants changing behaviors that ultimately lead to improved business metrics.

Without behavioral change, the training course is meaningless. The participants can attend your four-hour training and receive a certificate. If they return to their daily operations without using the course content, it is a wasted four hours.

The participants can log out from the most engaging webinar, leaving comments on evaluations that they "really enjoyed" the session or "the material was relevant." But if they do not implement what you taught, the webinar did not meet its objective.

You can use pre-tests and post-tests to show that the participants learned information. But if they never implement what they learned, their knowledge will not yield results.

Meaningful training occurs when participants master new skills and apply the skills to their day-to-day operations. Practical application of course content is the goal of a dynamic facilitator.

Facilitating training in a virtual environment contains many of the same elements as in-person training. However, the facilitator must thoughtfully execute the instruction in a virtual environment. The strategies discussed in the guide provide a framework for developing a highly dynamic course.

Starting with the end—the why or the value—sets up the trajectory of the course. Establishing the purpose first is critical to designing the course. Whether you are an expert or have imposter's syndrome, it is encouraging to remember that the course is not about your performance. You are there to guide your participants to meet the course objectives. Establishing this mindset can take the pressure off of you to feel that you have to perform or entertain. It also enables you to design the course with the participants' success as your goal. With a few intentional strategies, you can create a distraction-free and welcoming environment that eases participant tension and establishes an optimal setting for engaged learning. Facilitating activities in a virtual setting can be intimidating. However, there are simple ideas to keep your participants' attention and guide them through active learning exercises in a virtual environment.

It takes creativity to deliver a smooth course virtually with both active and passive teaching strategies. Well-designed PowerPoints and recorded or live virtual white-board charting can be an effective way to present ideas and data visually. A variety of applications and technology can be used for participants to discuss, collaborate, share ideas, and create solutions. Social media platforms provide additional means of interactions and real-world applications.

You can feel less overwhelmed when you use an intentional strategy to design an online course. Plan what you will focus on before, during, and after the session with the 3-phase course design. Considering the course goals, you can decide how students will master the course objectives. Pre-work is an effective method to communicate the value of the course, introduce yourself, and have participants review the material ahead of time. Opening with a bang and establishing the why will energize the participants and create an environment conducive for active learning. Organizing the session and activities into an opening, the content, and the closing provides a consistent structure throughout the course. Explaining the why, what, and how for sessions and activities seamlessly communicates goals, objectives, and instructions. Planning becomes less intimidating when you think in twenty-minute segments and alternate a variety of active and passive activities. A crucial aspect of the course involves the support you and the supervisors offer to the participants. Strategic assessments will help you determine the impact of the training on business metrics and justify the value of the course.

Effective training culminates in the participants changing behaviors that ultimately leads to improved business metric

---

Facilitating through a screen can be intimidating. However, if you consciously focus on a few presenting and speaking techniques, you will lead with ease. Participants might think it will be easy to hide behind their screens, but there are several methods you can use to avoid the dreaded silence and foster enthusiastic engagement. As you become more confident in your facilitating skills, you will be able to cater to varied learning preferences and adapt your course to meet your participants' learning needs.

It is not likely that any course will run flawlessly. However, there are ways to approach facilitating challenges with confidence. Being aware of a few strategies for handling unexpected glitches can reduce the fear of leading a virtual course. You may have resistant participants. Listen to uncover the underlying cause of the resistance and demonstrate the value of the content for them. The most crucial aspect of training is for the participants to change their behavior in their day-to-day operations. To gain their trust, they have to see that the organization supports the implementation of the material taught.

If you execute the training well, the business should expect to see dividends from the course—if the participants understand the course value, visualize the connection between the content and business metrics, engage in the learning process, master skills through active learning, and implement course content. Facilitating this kind of exceptional training in a virtual environment requires effort. However, just like any other skill, you will improve each time you practice. Start by choosing a few strategies in this book. Implement, reflect, adapt, and try again. In no time at all, you will become a dynamic facilitator!

References

References are listed numerically in the order they appear in the text. References that are repeated throughout the book are listed only under the strategy in which they were first cited.

Introduction
1. Kirkpatrick, J. D., & Kirkpatrick W. K. (2016). *Kirkpatrick's four levels of training evaluation* (1st ed.). Alexandria, VA: Association for Talent Development.
2. Knowles, M. S. (1978, January). Andragogy: Adult learning theory in perspective. *Community College Review, 5*(3), 9-20. doi:10.1177/009155217800500302
3. Merriam, S. G. (2008, Fall). Adult learning theory for the twenty-first century (3rd Update, Special Issue). *New Directions for Adult and Continuing Education, 2008*(119), 93-98. doi:10.1002/ace.309
4. Merriam, S. B. (2001, Spring). Andragogy and self-direct learning: Pillars of adult learning theory (Special Issue). *New Directions for Adult and Continuing Education, 2001*(89), 3-19. doi:10.1002/ace.3
5. Krathwohl, D. R. (2010, June). A revision of Bloom's taxonomy: An overview. *Theory into Practice, 41*(4), 212-218. doi:10.1207/s15430421tip4104_2
6. Mancuso, D. S., Chlup, D. T., & McWhorter, R. R. (2010, December). A study of adult learning in a virtual world. *Advances in Developing Human Resources, 12*(6), 681-699. doi:10.1177/1523422310395368

Strategy 1
7. Armstrong, P. (2001). *Bloom's taxonomy, Figure.* Nashville, TN: Vanderbilt University Center for Teaching. Retrieved from https://cft.vanderbilt.edu/guides-sub-pages/blooms-taxonomy/
8. Schinkel, S. L. (2019, March 14). *How do I love Bloom's taxonomy? Let me count the ways* [Blog post]. Port Melbourne,

Australia: Center for Organization Development, My Growth Mindset. Retrieved from https://mygrowthmindset.home.blog/2019/03/14/how-do-i-love-blooms-taxonomy-let-me-count-the-ways/

Strategy 5

9. Geri, N., Winer, A., & Zaks, B. (2017, May). Challenging the six-minute myth of online lectures: Can interactivity expand the attention span of learners? *Online Journal of Applied Knowledge Management, 5*(1), 101-111. doi:10.36965/OJAKM.2017.5(1)101-111

Strategy 6

10. Chi, M. T. H., & Wylie, R. (2014, October). The ICAP framework: Linking cognitive engagement to active learning outcomes. *Educational Psychologist, 49*(4), 219-243. doi:10.1080/00461520.2014.965823

11. Freeman, S., Eddy, S. L., McDonough, M., Smith, M. K., Okoroafor, N., Jordt, H., & Wenderoth, M. P. (2014, June). Active learning increases student performance in science, engineering, and mathematics. *Proceedings of the National Academy of Sciences in the United States of America, 111*(23), 8410-8415. doi:10.1073/pnas.1319030111

12. Markant, D. B., Ruggeri, A., Gureckis, T. M., & Xu, F. (2016, September). Enhanced memory as a common effect of active learning (Special Issue). *Mind, Brain, and Education Society, 10*(3), 142-152. doi:10.1111/mbe.12117

13. Khan, A., Egbue, O., Palkie, B., & Madden, J. (2017). Active learning: Engaging students to maximize learning in an online course. *Electronic Journal of e-Learning, 15*(2), 107-115. Retrieved from https://files.eric.ed.gov/fulltext/EJ1141876.pdf

14. NTL Institute for Applied Behavioral Science. (1954). *The learning pyramid.* Bethel, ME: NTL Institute for Applied Behavioral Science.

15. de Bono, E. (1999). *Six thinking hats* (2nd ed.). New York, NY: Little and Brown.

Strategy 17

16. Dirksen, D. J. (2011, April). Hitting the resent button: Using formative assessment to guide instruction. *Phi Delta Kappan, 92*(7), 26-31. doi:10.1177/003172171109200706

17. WorkSmart. (2018). *Memorable debriefs* [Blog]. Natick, MA: WorkSmart. Retrieved from https://blog.trainerswarehouse.com/memorable-debriefing

Strategy 18

18. Benjamin, L. T., Jr. (2002). Lecturing. In S. F. Davis and W. Buskist (Eds.), *The teaching of psychology: Essays in honor of Wilbert J. McKeachie and Charles L. Brewer* (Chapter 5, pp. 57-67). Mahwah, NJ: Lawrence Erlbaum Associates.

19. Bradbury, N. A. (2016, December). Attention span during lectures: 8 seconds, 10 minutes, or more? *Advanced Physiology of Education, 40*(5), 509-513. doi:10.1152/advan.00109.2016

20. Miyaoka, J., Ozsen, L., Zhao, Y., & Cholette, S. (2018, December). Experiential undergraduate operation management course engages students. *Journal of Supply Chain and Operations Management, 16*(3), 219-245. Retrieved from https://www.csupom.com/uploads/1/1/4/8/114895679/16n3p1.pdf

Strategy 22

21. Beer, M., Finnström, M., & Schrader D. (2016, October). Why leadership training fails—And what to do about it. *Harvard Business Review,* 50-57. Retrieved from https://hbr.org/2016/10/why-leadership-training-fails-and-what-to-do-about-it

Strategy 29

22. Townsend, J. (2015). *Management pocketbooks*. Ferney-Voltaire, France: Master Trainer Institute. Retrieved from https://www.pocketbook.co.uk/media_mp/preview/978190661015 9(Preview).pdf

Appendix A: Course Design Review Checklist

You can use this checklist to evaluate the design elements of a current course or to review a course you have already created.

Strategy	Review Element	Yes/No	Notes For Improvement
1	I designed my course around the WHY—overall purpose—of the course.		
1	I wrote my course objectives with action verbs (I did not use "learn, understand, appreciate", etc.).		
2	I am more focused on guiding the participants toward the learning objectives rather than highlighting that I am the expert.		
3	I have established a distraction-free atmosphere (to the extent possible).		
4	There is a welcoming activity, song, or slide to greet participants.		
5	I use a variety of methods to keep the participants' attention.		
6	I included both active and passive learning strategies in my course.		
7	I am using appropriate technological platforms to deliver my course.		
8	My PowerPoints are not excessively wordy.		
8	I conduct some sessions or activities without a PowerPoint.		
9	I use a virtual whiteboard for some presentations or activities.		
10	I have thoughtfully and carefully used social media in my course (if applicable).		
11	I use the three-phase training design as I prepare my participants ahead of time, conduct the training, and then follow up with the participants after the course.		
12	I have pre-communication or pre-work that I use before my course.		
13	I open my course with a bang.		

14	I communicate the WHY of the course at the very beginning.		
15	I divided my course into sessions or modules, which are composed of a presentation of teaching content and active learning exercises.		
15	I have structured the course, sessions, and activities with an opening, content, and closing.		
15	I have clearly and concisely embedded the why, what, and how into every opening, content, and closing.		
16	I have a variety of active learning exercises throughout my course.		
17	I conduct a debrief in the closing of my activities, sessions, and the course.		
18	I maintain roughly a 60/40 ratio of active to passive learning strategies.		
19	I planned my activities in 20-minute segments.		
20	I "hit the sweet" spot as my course is not overly long, nor are participants rushed through course objectives they did not master.		
21	I have a strong close to my course.		
22	I follow up with my participants after the training.		
23	I assess the participants' satisfaction and engagement during and after the course.		
23	I assess the improvement in the participants' skills or knowledge throughout my course.		
23	I conduct follow up assessments 3-12 months after my course to evaluate a change in the participants' actions or behaviors in their work environment.		
23	I use short-term and longitudinal data to assess the impact of my training course on the related business metrics and the WHY of the course.		

Appendix B: Personal Facilitation Review Checklist

You can use this checklist to reflect and improve your facilitation style.

Strategy	Review Element	Yes/No	Notes For Improvement
25	I am not making excessive or repetitive motions with my hands or body while facilitating.		
25	I smile into the camera and look like I am enjoying myself.		
25	I vary the pace and intensity of my voice.		
26	I have a strategy to identify and reduce filler words.		
27	I am comfortable with silence after a question to allow the participants to formulate their answers.		
27	I have strategies to engage participants and prevent prolonged silence.		
28	I have a method to identify the participants' learning needs.		
28	I have built some flexibility into my course to adapt to the unique learning needs of different groups of participants.		
29	I have a plan to "throw the monkey" or make a joke if needed to ease a tense or awkward situation.		
30	I ask questions and listen to determine the underlying cause of a participants' resistance.		
30	I use the WHY of the course, personal application, and other strategies to reduce participants' resistance.		
31	I work with the organization's administration to ensure they provide support for the long-term application of the course material.		

Appendix C: Implement-Review-Improve-Repeat Reflection Guide

Facilitating is a skill. The more you facilitate, the better you will become. Use the Continued Improvement Model below to improve your course design and facilitation. Choose a few strategies from this guide to implement in your next course. After the class, review what worked well and what could be improved. You can use course evaluations and personal reflections to identify focus areas. Decide what action steps you can take to improve for the next course.

Implement
Which strategies did you try to implement? What did you add or modify in your course?

Review
How did the strategy work? On a scale of 1-10, how effective was it? How did you feel about the success or lack thereof? What worked well? What was difficult? Was there a barrier to implementing the strategy?

Improve
What will you do differently next time? What action steps do you need to take to improve? Describe how you will measure improvement. Set small goals and deadlines to make adjustments.

Repeat
Continue to implement, review, and reflect throughout your career as you progress toward becoming a learner-focused, dynamic, engaging, and effective facilitator.

About the Authors

Dr. Cara Cordrey Gomez

Dr. Cara Gomez (CEO and Owner of New Reality Leadership, LLC) is an Athletic Trainer, a healthcare provider for the physically active. She has a doctorate degree in Organizational Leadership from Wilmington University. She is currently an Assistant Professor at Delaware State University and has developed and teaches several online courses. Her research interests include leadership, pedagogy, and translational research. Dr. Gomez has a strong interest in measuring the effectiveness of both traditional and online  courses. Dr. Gomez develops assessments to measure business metrics and is interested in further researching the link between leadership skill development and business and health-related outcomes.

Neil Cordrey

Neil Cordrey (Founder and Owner of New Reality Leadership, LLC) has over forty years of leadership and coaching experience across manufacturing, retail, and food industries. He most recently worked at the DuPont company as a learning consultant. His career included a focus on technical and safety training, as well as career development and organizational culture transition.

Mr. Cordrey has witnessed companies overlooking leadership potential by doing one of three things:

promoting employees into managerial positions without training, having supervisors attend long "training" sessions without follow up, or providing development opportunities only for senior leaders. Additionally, he noticed that companies **rarely link leadership training to business output or performance.**

By observing departments with effective business performance and identifying the leaders' actions, Mr. Cordrey developed a suite of leadership development tools branded as New Reality Leadership. He began to coach leaders on these skills while tracking performance metrics specific to the business. Mr. Cordrey's leadership materials include real case studies and examples. They are easy to implement across all levels of the organization. When applied correctly, the New Reality Leadership principles have a profound impact on business outcomes.

Photo Credit: David Powlosin

About New Reality Leadership

New Reality Leadership is a leadership coaching and consulting agency.

Simplifying the leadership approach, **New Reality focuses on effective and accelerated leadership skill development to improve business metrics**. New Reality Leadership helps businesses **foster strong leadership throughout the entire company**—from senior leadership to front line employees—to maximize performance and profitability.

New Reality Leadership concentrates on two aspects of leadership development rarely emphasized by other companies: linking the leadership training to business metrics and providing interactive, ongoing skill development coaching.

> **Linking leadership training to business performance.** New Reality Leadership coaches businesses to not look at leadership development as an item to check off a checklist for employees. Instead, the company should be able to identify how the skills and behaviors improve business performance. A business first determines business improvement focus areas and metrics specific to those improvements. Leaders connect how the skills and actions influence the impact on the mission, vision, and production of the unit. One New Reality Leadership client demonstrated a 47% increase in production in two years. There was minimal improvement during the previous five years before using the New Reality approach.

> **Ongoing skill development and assessing improvement.** New Reality Leadership does not view their training as "one-time" retreats or sessions. Content and coaching are presented regularly over time. Skills are introduced, assessed, practiced, and mastered.

Leaders are encouraged to practice skills, reflect on challenges and successes, and continuously improve behaviors.

New Reality Leadership offers a suite of leadership development resources that can be customized and scaled for varying-sized companies and business needs. The resources, which can be modified for facilitator preference and are easy to use, include facilitator guides, PowerPoints for in-person sessions, self-study guides, and participant workbooks. Discussion guides and other resources are available for Senior Leaders. New Reality also offers assessment tools or can custom-create assessments to evaluate business metrics specific to a company or individual department. Coaching support is available for leaders at all levels and includes virtual coaching, on-site coaching, train-the-trainer, and instructional design support.